EXPLORING THE STATES

New Jersey

THE GARDEN STATE

by Hannah Rogal

BELLWETHER MEDIA • MINNEAPOLIS, MN

Note to Librarians, Teachers, and Parents:

Blastoff! Readers are carefully developed by literacy experts and combine standards-based content with developmentally appropriate text.

Level 1 provides the most support through repetition of high-frequency words, light text, predictable sentence patterns, and strong visual support.

Level 2 offers early readers a bit more challenge through varied simple sentences, increased text load, and less repetition of high-frequency words.

Level 3 advances early-fluent readers toward fluency through increased text and concept load, less reliance on visuals, longer sentences, and more literary language.

Level 4 builds reading stamina by providing more text per page, increased use of punctuation, greater variation in sentence patterns, and increasingly challenging vocabulary.

Level 5 encourages children to move from "learning to read" to "reading to learn" by providing even more text, varied writing styles, and less familiar topics.

Whichever book is right for your reader, Blastoff! Readers are the perfect books to build confidence and encourage a love of reading that will last a lifetime!

This edition first published in 2014 by Bellwether Media, Inc.

No part of this publication may be reproduced in whole or in part without written permission of the publisher. For information regarding permission, write to Bellwether Media, Inc., Attention: Permissions Department, 5357 Penn Avenue South, Minneapolis, MN 55419.

Library of Congress Cataloging-in-Publication Data

Rogal, Hannah.
  New Jersey / by Hannah Rogal.
    pages cm. – (Blastoff! readers. Exploring the states)
  Includes bibliographical references and index.
  Summary: "Developed by literacy experts for students in grades three through seven, this book introduces young readers to the geography and culture of New Jersey"– Provided by publisher.
  ISBN 978-1-62617-029-2 (hardcover : alk. paper)
  1. New Jersey–Juvenile literature. I. Title.
  F134.3.R64 2014
  974.9–dc23
                                              2013004892

Table of Contents

Where Is New Jersey?

New Jersey is a small, crowded state on the East Coast of the United States. Its capital, Trenton, sits in the middle of the state's western border.

Water surrounds most of New Jersey. The Delaware River separates the state from Pennsylvania and Delaware in the west. The Atlantic Ocean washes onto the southern and eastern shores. The Hudson River forms the eastern border with New York. Only the state's short northern border with New York crosses land.

Did you know?
New Jersey was named after the British island of Jersey. It lies in the English Channel between England and France.

Maryland

4

New York

Hudson River

Delaware River

Paterson ●

Newark ● ● Jersey City

Great Swamp
National
Wildlife Refuge

★ Trenton

Pennsylvania

New Jersey

Atlantic
Ocean

Delaware

N
W E
S

History

The Lenni Lenape Indians were the first people to live in what would become New Jersey. In 1524, Giovanni da Verrazzano was the first European to explore the area. More than 100 battles took place in New Jersey during the **Revolutionary War**. After the American victory, the state quickly became a center of growth and production.

fun fact

In the late 1870s, Thomas Edison worked in a science lab in Menlo Park. It was here that he perfected the lightbulb.

New Jersey Timeline!

1524:	**European explorer Giovanni da Verrazzano reaches the New Jersey area.**
1609:	**Henry Hudson arrives in Sandy Hook Bay. He claims the area for the Netherlands.**
1776:	**George Washington leads troops to a key victory in the Revolutionary War at the Battle of Trenton.**
1787:	**New Jersey becomes the third state.**
1846:	**The first professional baseball game is played in Hoboken.**
1912:	**Woodrow Wilson, a New Jersey governor, is elected the twenty-eighth President of the United States.**
1951:	**The New Jersey Turnpike opens. It becomes a busy national highway.**
2012:	**Hurricane Sandy strikes the entire East Coast. Floodwaters destroy many towns along the Jersey Shore.**

Hurricane Sandy damage

Woodrow Wilson

New Jersey Turnpike

New Jersey's land varies greatly. In the northwest stand the Kittatinny Mountains. The Delaware River cuts through their peaks along the Pennsylvania border. On the other side of the state, rocky cliffs line the Hudson River.

Cities and **suburbs** pack the northern portion of New Jersey. Roads cross over rivers and wrap around hundreds of ponds and lakes. The low, flat **plain** of the south is less crowded. Dazzling beaches line the Atlantic coast. **Salt marshes**, pine forests, and small farms and orchards lie inland.

salt marsh

New Jersey's Climate

average °F

spring
Low: 42°
High: 61°

summer
Low: 65°
High: 83°

fall
Low: 47°
High: 66°

winter
Low: 26°
High: 43°

Did you know?
New Jersey was nicknamed the Garden State in the 1800s. Back then, New Jersey farms produced a bounty of vegetables for New York and Pennsylvania.

Great Swamp National Wildlife Refuge

great blue
heron

Tucked inside the suburbs of northern New Jersey is a
unique area of wilderness. The Great Swamp National
Wildlife Refuge was created in 1960 to protect animal
habitats. More than 8 miles (13 kilometers) of hiking trails
take nature lovers through wetlands. Here, trees and grasses
grow out of the murky water. The trails also pass through
meadows, woods, and streams.

wood turtle

Around 26 threatened or **endangered** animal species live in the refuge. The rare wood turtle makes its home in streams and nearby woodlands. The wetlands also serve as a rest stop for more than 240 **migrating** bird species.

Wildlife

Many kinds of birds swoop and flit through New Jersey's skies. The majestic great blue heron glides along the coast in search of prey. Inland, bird-watchers listen for the whistle of the Baltimore oriole. This sound is a sure sign that spring is on its way. Violets, lilies, buttercups, and other wildflowers will soon bloom everywhere.

Maple, birch, and oak trees fill the state's forests and backyards. In fall, the leaves turn bright shades of red, orange, and yellow. Deer and black bears roam through the forests. Squirrels, opossums, and raccoons are common sights in both woodlands and cities.

black bear

Baltimore oriole

opossum

Landmarks

Atlantic City is a seaside **resort** that feels like a carnival. **Casinos** with dazzling lights lure gamblers to their card tables. Ocean lovers crowd the beautiful beaches. They stroll the bustling **boardwalk** that runs along the shore.

Historic Cape May is another city on the sea. Its old lighthouse still guides ships today. Visitors can climb 199 steps to the top and look out over Delaware Bay. Morristown National Historical Park is a must-see for history fans. During the Revolutionary War, George Washington and his troops survived a bitterly cold winter there.

Cape May lighthouse

Morristown National Historical Park

Did you know?

All the property names in the game Monopoly are names of real streets in Atlantic City.

Atlantic City

Newark

Newark is the largest city in New Jersey. It lies on Newark Bay, just 10 miles (16 kilometers) west of New York City. Newark is a major hub for airlines, trains, and trucking companies. Hundreds of cargo ships sail into its **port** every year.

Branch Brook Park is Newark's largest park. It has more than 4,000 cherry blossom trees. They bloom in April and attract visitors from all over the world.

Many **immigrants** move to Newark with the promise of work. The city's **diversity** is reflected in its **ethnic** restaurants and food trucks. These kitchens on wheels serve tacos and pita wraps to go. At Branch Brook Park, people eat lunch under a pink haze of cherry blossom trees.

Working

In the 1800s, New Jersey workers built roadways, railroads, and **canals**. These allowed businesses to sell and ship their products. Factories grew as immigrants came in search of work. Today, New Jersey is a leading producer of chemicals, electronics, and food products.

New Jersey is also a center of research. Many of its workers are scientists or **engineers**. Most New Jerseyans have **service jobs**. They work in banks, hospitals, and schools. Farms cover about one-sixth of the state. Garden State farmers are famous for their prize peaches and blueberries.

Where People Work in New Jersey

manufacturing
6%

farming and
natural resources
1%

government
13%

services
80%

Playing

New Jersey's varied landscape offers many opportunities for outdoor fun. Swimmers and surfers gather on the Jersey Shore, which is famous for its big waves. Hikers trek around the lakes and mountains in the north.

Cultural activities are also popular. The Newark Museum is the largest museum in the state. Here, families can learn about the planets or view art from around the world. The New Jersey Performing Arts Center is one of the busiest in the country. The center is home to the New Jersey Symphony Orchestra. It also hosts **Broadway** musicals.

Newark Museum

fun fact !

Some people call New Jersey the Diner Capital of the World. Its many diners dish cheap burgers and milkshakes in a fun, casual setting.

surfing

Food

lobster roll

steamed clams with butter

Food in New Jersey is diverse, just like the people. Italian, Cuban, and Portuguese dishes are common. Italian hot dogs are one favorite. They come inside chewy buns made from pizza dough. The hot dogs are topped with peppers, onions, and potatoes. Tomato pie is another famous dish. It is like pizza, but the sauce is poured on top of the cheese.

Fresh seafood can be found everywhere in New Jersey. Many restaurants serve lobster rolls in the summer. These sandwiches are stuffed with a mixture of lobster meat, mayonnaise, and celery. Steamed clams dipped in melted butter are another tasty treat.

Salt Water Taffy

Ingredients:

- 1 cup white sugar
- 1/4 cup light corn syrup
- 2/3 cup water
- 2 tablespoons butter
- 1 tablespoon cornstarch
- 1 teaspoon salt
- 1 teaspoon of your favorite flavor extract
- Food coloring (optional)

! fun fact

Salt water taffy was first made in Atlantic City. This soft, chewy candy comes in many fun flavors.

Directions:

1. Grease one 8-inch baking pan.

2. In a 2-quart saucepan over medium heat, combine all ingredients except flavor and color. Mix well and bring to a boil.

3. Heat without stirring until candy thermometer reads 255°F (124°C).

4. Remove from heat. Stir in flavor and color, if desired. Pour into baking pan.

5. Let stand until cool enough to handle. (Taffy should be lukewarm throughout.)

6. Lightly grease hands. Form a big ball, then fold, double, and pull the taffy until it is light in color and stiff.

7. Roll into a long rope. Then cut taffy into pieces with greased scissors. Wrap pieces with wax paper.

Festivals

Festival of Ballooning

Every July, the sky above Readington fills with colorful hot air balloons. More than 150,000 people flock to the New Jersey Festival of Ballooning. Visitors can go on balloon rides or see live concerts and fireworks. One highlight is a display of floating animals, famous characters, and other specially shaped balloons.

Miss America 2013

In June, Newark's Portugal Day Festival attracts thousands with live music, ethnic food, and kids' activities. In Hudson County, people line the streets for the yearly Cuban Parade. Roaring motorcycles, marching bands, and colorful floats pass through the cheering crowds.

Ellis Island

Ellis Island is often thought to be part of New York. In fact, most of it belongs to New Jersey. Ellis Island was the first stop for many immigrants coming to the United States. From 1892 to 1924, some 12 million people landed on its shores. They hoped to start a new life in America.

On the island, officers interviewed immigrants and tested their health. Those who passed were allowed to live in the United States. Today, **tourists** can visit the Ellis Island Immigration Museum. It honors those who helped build New Jersey and the nation.

fun fact

Most of the people who passed through Ellis Island came from Eastern and Southern Europe. About two out of every five Americans are related to someone who arrived on Ellis Island.

Fast Facts About New Jersey

New Jersey's Flag

New Jersey's state flag is tan and blue. George Washington chose the colors for the state's army during the Revolutionary War. The coat of arms is in the center. It features a shield with three plows. They represent farming in the state. On each side of the shield stands a goddess. They represent the state motto.

State Flower
common blue violet

State Nickname:	The Garden State
State Motto:	"Liberty and Prosperity"
Year of Statehood:	1787
Capital City:	Trenton
Other Major Cities:	Newark, Jersey City, Paterson
Population:	8,791,894 (2010)
Area:	7,812 square miles (20,233 square kilometers); New Jersey is the 47th largest state.
Major Industries:	tourism, research, chemical manufacturing
Natural Resources:	sand, stone, soil, fish
State Government:	80 representatives; 40 senators
Federal Government:	12 representatives; 2 senators
Electoral Votes:	14

State Animal
horse

State Bird
eastern goldfinch

29

Glossary

boardwalk—a raised sidewalk made of wood, steel, or concrete; boardwalks often run along beaches.

Broadway—professional theater based in New York City

canals—waterways that are usually built to connect larger bodies of water

casinos—buildings where people bet money on games of chance

diversity—variety of cultures or backgrounds

endangered—at risk of becoming extinct

engineers—workers who use science and math to solve problems or create advanced technology

ethnic—from another country or cultural background

immigrants—people who leave one country to live in another country

migrating—traveling from one place to another, often with the seasons

plain—a large area of flat land

port—a sea harbor where ships can dock

resort—a vacation spot that offers recreation, entertainment, and relaxation

Revolutionary War—the war between 1775 and 1783 in which the United States fought for independence from Great Britain

salt marshes—coastal wetlands that are often flooded with saltwater

service jobs—jobs that perform tasks for people or businesses

suburbs—communities that lie just outside a city

tourists—people who travel to visit another place

wildlife refuge—a natural area in which wildlife is protected

To Learn More

AT THE LIBRARY

McDaniel, Melissa. *Ellis Island*. New York, N.Y.: Children's Press, 2011.

Murphy, Jim. *The Crossing: How George Washington Saved the American Revolution*. New York, N.Y.: Scholastic Press, 2010.

Nault, Jennifer. *New Jersey: The Garden State*. New York, N.Y.: Weigl, 2012.

ON THE WEB

Learning more about New Jersey is as easy as 1, 2, 3.

1. Go to www.factsurfer.com.

2. Enter "New Jersey" into the search box.

3. Click the "Surf" button and you will see a list of related Web sites.

With factsurfer.com, finding more information is just a click away.

Index

The images in this book are reproduced through the courtesy of: cdrin, front cover; (Collection)/ Prints & Photographs Division/ Library of Congress, pp. 6, 7 (middle); Leonard Zhukovsky, p. 7 (left); DougSchneiderPhoto, p. 7 (right); Minden Pictures/ SuperStock, p. 8 (small); gary718, pp. 8-9; Samuel R. Maglione/ Getty Images, pp. 10-11; Ryan M. Bolton, p. 11 (top); Skip Brown/ Getty Images, p. 11 (bottom); Critterbiz, p. 12 (top); Gerald A. DeBoer, p. 12 (middle); rthoma, p. 12 (bottom); Fadyukhin, pp. 12-13; Racheal Grazias, p. 14 (top); Spirit of America, p. 14 (bottom); SeanPavonePhoto, pp. 14-15; DenisTangneyJr, pp. 16-17; AP Photo/ Mike Derer, p. 17; Clay McLachla/ Getty Images, p. 18; Pressmaster, p. 19; AP Photo/ Mike Derer, p. 20 (top); andipantz, p. 20 (bottom); Andrew F. Kazmierski, pp. 20-21; Margoe Edwards, p. 22; FoodCollection/ SuperStock, p. 22 (small); GWImages p. 23; AP Photo/ Mel Evans, pp. 24-25; AP Photo/ Isaac Brekken, p. 25 (small); SeanPavonePhoto, pp. 26-27; Richard Green/ Alamy, p. 27 (small); Pakmor, p. 28 (top); Charles Brutlag, p. 28 (bottom); Stephen Bonk, p. 29 (left); Eric Isselee, p. 29 (right).

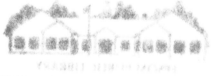

THE SINKING OF THE USS *MAINE*

DECLARING WAR AGAINST SPAIN

MILESTONES
IN
AMERICAN HISTORY

THE SINKING OF
THE USS *MAINE*

DECLARING WAR AGAINST SPAIN

SAMUEL WILLARD CROMPTON

CHELSEA HOUSE
PUBLISHERS

An imprint of Infobase Publishing

The Sinking of the USS *Maine*

Copyright © 2009 by Infobase Publishing

Chelsea House
An imprint of Infobase Publishing
132 West 31st Street
New York NY 10001

Library of Congress Cataloging-in-Publication Data
Crompton, Samuel Willard.
  The sinking of the USS Maine : declaring war against Spain / Samuel Willard Crompton.
  p. cm. — (Milestones in American history)
  Includes bibliographical references and index.
  ISBN 978–1-60413–049–2 (hardcover)
  1. Maine (Battleship) 2. Spanish-American War, 1898—Causes. 3. Cuba—History—Revolution, 1895–1898. I. Title. II. Series.
  E721.6.C88 2008
  973.8'9—dc22   2008025309

Series design by Erik Lindstrom
Cover design by Ben Peterson

Printed in the United States of America

Bang NMSG 10 9 8 7 6 5 4 3 2 1

This book is printed on acid-free paper.

All links and Web addresses were checked and verified to be correct at the time of publication. Because of the dynamic nature of the Web, some addresses and links may have changed since publication and may no longer be valid.

CONTENTS

With the Wounded

"Suddenly the sounds of a terrific explosion shook the city."

—*An American journalist in Havana*

Clara Barton was among the best-known of all nineteenth century American women. Called the Angel of the Battlefield, she had tended the sick and wounded after numerous Civil War engagements, including Antietam, in which more than 30,000 men were killed or wounded.

Barton turned 76 on December 25, 1897. She had worked hard all her life, but she was not ready to retire. Another war was raging in Cuba, and the American National Red Cross, which Barton had founded, was needed there. Although Barton had just returned from a trip to Armenia, where the Armenians were fighting the Turks, she agreed to go to Cuba to direct relief operations. Before she left, she met with President William McKinley, who blessed her efforts and gave a personal donation of $5,000 to the Cuban International Relief Committee. A modest man, the president did not disclose his contribution to the press; the public learned of it many years later, after his death. Clara Barton arrived in Havana on February 9, 1898.

THE LADY AND THE CAPTAIN

Captain Charles Dwight Sigsbee, commander of the USS *Maine*, had arrived in Havana two weeks earlier. Responding first to a signal from the American consul in Havana and then to direct orders from the U.S. Navy, Captain Sigsbee brought the battleship *Maine* down from Key West, just 90 miles (144.8 kilometers) away. When he arrived in Havana Harbor on January 25, he found the city relatively quiet.

Captain Sigsbee knew that the situation could change at any time, for Havana—indeed, all of Cuba—had been in a state of war for almost three years. Native-born Cubans had risen in revolt against Spanish rule in 1895, and the island had experienced a great deal of blood and suffering since. The U.S. Navy sent Captain Sigsbee and the *Maine* to demonstrate American power in the region, to let both rebels and imperial troops know that America would protect its citizens in Havana. Within days of his arrival, Captain Sigsbee telegraphed Washington that, in his opinion, the presence of the battleship allowed the United States to exercise a dominant position in the region (at least in the area covered by its mighty guns).

How the people of Havana felt was another matter. The many Spanish-born Cubans in the city looked upon the battleship *Maine* as a threat and a suggestion of Yankee imperialism. One day, as Captain Sigsbee went to a bullfight in the city, he had a leaflet thrust upon him. Ranting against the presence of the American ship and the weakness of some in the Spanish government, the leaflet called for "death to the Americans!"

Clara Barton, the "Angel of the Battlefield," is shown here in 1904 at the age of 83. She retired that year from the American chapter of the Red Cross, which she had founded. She died in April 1912.

Ever unflappable, the captain put the leaflet in his pocket and forgot about it.

On Sunday, February 13, Captain Sigsbee invited Clara Barton to come aboard the *Maine*. Born in 1845, he was a full generation younger than she, but he knew her story very well, as did most Americans. Sigsbee had served in the Civil War after graduating from the Naval Academy at Annapolis in 1863, and he knew that Barton had been one of the most instrumental figures of that great conflict. Barton accepted Sigsbee's invitation and, sometime in the early afternoon, she went aboard the *Maine.*

There were no photographs nor any record of their conversation, but we can imagine the manner with which the captain and the lady conducted themselves. Clara Barton and Captain Sigsbee were both American Victorians, and they took their social cues from Britain's Queen Victoria, who had acceded to the English throne when Barton was only 16 years old. Victorian gentlemen like Captain Sigsbee wore neatly pressed trousers, high starched collars, and hats; few men of the time allowed themselves to be photographed bare-headed. Victorian ladies like Clara Barton wore long tapered skirts (usually black), leather shoes, and high-collared blouses. Ladies wore hats and white gloves, too.

We cannot be certain about their conversation, but we imagine that Captain Sigsbee gave Barton a tour of the clean, swept deck of the *Maine,* though not of its grimy, soot-infested hold. Although she had spent a lifetime in the service of sick and wounded soldiers, Barton often confessed a weakness for some of the trappings of military and naval power. The *Maine,* with its turrets, guns, and engines, must have made a strong and positive impression. Few Victorian ladies went on board battleships in those days, and Clara Barton may well have savored the moment.

Barton and Captain Sigsbee probably discussed the condition of the people of Havana. Barton had arrived only four days earlier and did not know all of the details, but she was convinced that the *reconcentradros,* the unfortunate civilians rounded up by the Spanish troops and placed in concentration

CAPT. CHARLES D. SIGSBEE,
COMMANDER OF THE U. S. BATTLESHIP MAINE.

The captain of the USS *Maine*, Charles D. Sigsbee, was a graduate of the United States Naval Academy and served in the latter stages of the American Civil War. In 1897, he was appointed to the command of the *Maine*. Sigsbee retired in 1907 with the rank of rear admiral in command of the second squadron of the U.S. Atlantic Fleet.

camps, had suffered the most as a result of the Spanish-Cuban War. She had come to help those people in particular. Captain Sigsbee may have been sympathetic to their plight, but as a Navy officer, his mission was to keep the peace in Havana Harbor, not to assist the victims of the war.

All we know for certain about the conversation is that Miss Barton spoke with another officer, the second-in-command of the *Maine*, and she offered him and his men her assistance if anything should happen to them. Barton's primary mission was to help the victims of the war, but she was a patriotic American who would surely help her countrymen if there was any need. The officer's response is not recorded, but we imagine he smiled a bit, for what danger could befall the *Maine*? Going ashore, Barton returned to her work.

TAPS

Two days later, on the evening of February 15, Captain Sigsbee retired to his cabin to write a letter. At one point, he wrote to his wife that he heard the bugler play "Taps," the song of nightfall, and felt his usual pleasure at the melodious quality of the notes. Then, at 9:40 P.M., the force of an explosion startled him:

> It was a bursting, rending, and crashing sound or roar of immense volume, largely metallic in its character. It was succeeded by a metallic sound—probably of falling debris—a trembling and lurching motion of the vessel, then an impression of subsidence [sinking of land level], attended by an eclipse of the electric lights [the *Maine* was one of the first American warships to have electric lights].[1]

Captain Sigsbee stumbled out of his cabin and headed for the deck.

Back ashore, Clara Barton was hard at work. She and a fellow American, who was a member of the Cuban International Relief Committee, were going over papers, expenses, and receipts. These had always been the bane of her existence; like many other high-strung and excitable people, she was far better in the heat of a conflict than in dealing with clerical matters.

> [We were] busy at our writing tables until late at night. The house had grown still; the noises on the street were dying away, when suddenly the table shook from under our hands, the great glass door opening on to the veranda, facing the sea, flew open; everything in the room was in motion or out of place—the deafening roar of such a burst of thunder as perhaps never one heard before, and off to the right, out over the bay, the air was filled with a blaze of light, and this in turn filled with black specks light huge specters flying in all directions. . . . I supposed it to be the bursting of some mammoth mortar or explosion of some magazine.[2]

It was, in fact, the *Maine*.

George Bronson Rea, another American observer on shore that night, was a journalist for *Harper's Weekly*. He had been in Cuba for almost two years and in his recent book, *Facts and Fakes About Cuba*, he was much more sympathetic to the Spanish point of view than most American journalists. In fact, he had accused his fellow writers of staying in Havana rather than going to the countryside to see what was truly happening. This night, however, he was at a Havana café when he, too, heard the mighty blast: "Suddenly the sounds of a terrific explosion shook the city; windows were broken, and doors were shaken from their bolts. The sky towards the bay was lit up with an intense light, and above it all could be seen innumerable colored lights resembling rockets."[3]

In such a circumstance, many people would run for cover, but Rea and another American journalist hastened to the waterfront, where they found barricades. They told the Spaniards that they were officers of the *Maine*, a bold-faced lie that helped Rea and the other American get into a boat with the Havana chief of police. Commanding the oarsmen to row toward the *Maine*, the police captain and the two Americans had to use a cane and a rope to make them comply. Rea described the scene: "Great masses of twisted and bent iron plates and beams were thrown up in confusion amidships; the bow had disappeared; the fore-mast and smoke-stacks had fallen; and to add to the horror and danger, the mass of wreckage amidships was on fire."[4] The *Maine* was clearly sinking. What happened to its crew?

IN THE HOSPITAL

Clara Barton was late to the scene because she thought that the great explosion had been on land, or that it had been some sort of demonstration of military power. Although she was not present when the *Maine* went down, she did reach the Ambrosia Hospital in time to give aid and comfort to the wounded. On her way from her hotel to the hospital, she met the second-in-command of the *Maine*, who sadly asked if she remembered her pledge of two days earlier: that she would be available to the crew in case of a disaster. She certainly did recall, and the memory pushed her on to the Ambrosia Hospital where she found

> thirty to forty wounded—bruised, cut, burned; they had been crushed by timbers, cut by iron, scorched by fire, and blown sometimes high in the air, sometimes driven down through the red-hot furnace room and out into the water, senseless, to be picked up by some boat and gotten ashore. Their wounds are all over them—heads and faces terribly cut, internal wounds, arms, legs, feet, and hands burned to the live flesh.[5]

Although she was certainly familiar with disaster, Clara Barton had not witnessed a scene like this before. The Civil War wounded that she tended had experienced bullet wounds and shrapnel from cannon fire, but not the searing flames that

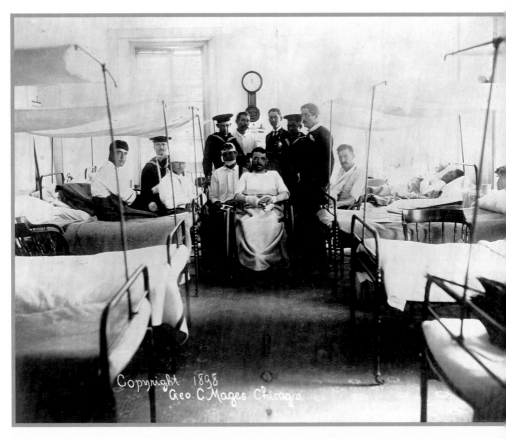

Copyright 1898
Geo. C. Mages Chicago.

Survivors of the USS *Maine* explosion pose for a picture at the Marine Hospital, where Clara Barton ministered to them, on February 21, 1898.

come from explosions and electrical fires. If this was war—and who was to say it was not?—it was a new type of war.

Barton did all she could for the men, sending telegrams on their behalf and staying with them that night. Sometime during that night she sent a telegram of her own to President William McKinley, who had urged her to go to Cuba in the first place. Her words were simple and to the point: "I am with the wounded."[6]

We do not know what the president's reaction to her telegram was, but we are confident that thousands, if not millions, of Americans were cheered to learn that the Civil War heroine was in action once more, tending to the wounded as she had done after the terrible battles of 1861–1865. A major poet of the day took her brief five-word missive and converted it into a song that the newspapers reprinted from coast to coast:

> *"I am with the wounded," flashed along the wire*
> *From the Isle of Cuba, swept with sword and fire.*
> *Angel sweet of mercy, may your cross of red*
> *Cheer the wounded living; bless the wounded dead.*
>
> *"I am with the starving," let the message run*
> *From this stricken island, when this task is done;*
> *Food and plenty wait at your command,*
> *Give in generous measure; fill each outstretched hand.*
>
> *"I am with the happy," this we long to hear*
> *From the Isle of Cuba, trembling now in fear;*
> *Make this great disaster touch the hearts of men,*
> *And, in God's great mercy, bring back peace again.*[7]

If there was to be war, it would be a new type of war. Americans, however, were thrilled to learn of the continuity Clara Barton would provide between the Civil War and what might now become the Spanish–American-Cuban War. Seventy-six-year-old Clara Barton had proved her worth once more.

The Gay Nineties

"Since the days when the fleet of Columbus sailed into the waters of the New World, America has been another name for opportunity."

—Frederick Jackson Turner, "The Significance of the
Frontier in American History"

The "Gay Nineties," which is how many people later described the years 1890–1900 in the United States, were not gay or happy for the laborers in tenements or for the farmers who went hungry in the Depression of 1893. Such expressions, however, usually are somewhat true. If the 1890s were not happy for everyone, there were many people alive at the time who felt they were or who hoped they might become so.

PROPHETS

As the 1890s advanced, Americans became increasingly aware that this, the last decade of the nineteenth century, might lead to surprising change. A number of prophets arose, some of them charlatans and some of them people of surpassing brilliance. Two of these men were Alfred Thayer Mahan and Frederick Jackson Turner.

Born in New York in 1840, Alfred Thayer Mahan was the son of a faculty member at the U.S. Military Academy at West Point. Although he was blessed with a fine brain, he was cursed with an immense ego, which would create difficulties many times during his life. Mahan made few friends during his college years and even fewer during his long service in the U.S. Navy. He did, however, discover the makings of a second profession: writing naval history. His first major work focused on U.S. naval activity in the Gulf of Mexico during the Civil War, and his second was *The Influence of Sea Power upon History, 1660–1783.*

Published in 1890, *The Influence of Sea Power* became one of the most influential books of its time. Mahan wrote of the glory days of the Spanish, French, Dutch, and British empires and their great navies, but his message naturally appealed to advocates of naval power in his own time.

Mahan's theory was complex, but its message was unmistakable. The country with the biggest merchant marine would have the biggest and strongest navy because of the availability of sailors. The country most willing to pump money into its navy would be the one to dominate its local region, and the nation that identified maritime affairs as supremely important would become the most powerful in the world. Geography backed up Mahan's thesis, for the Earth is approximately 72 percent ocean and only 28 percent land. Land-based empires, such as Napoleon's, would almost always succumb to sea-based empires, such as Queen Victoria's Britain.

Not everyone liked Mahan's theory, but many American policy makers did. A small group of like-minded thinkers began

The author of *The Influence of Sea Power upon History, 1660–1783* (1890), Alfred Thayer Mahan argued that America's future as an industrial power depended on foreign markets for American products, and that a strong navy and merchant marine would give the United States access to these markets. Interventionists such as Theodore Roosevelt used Mahan's theories to push for a war against the Spanish in Cuba.

to congregate at social clubs in Washington, D.C., where they pondered the best way to achieve American maritime supremacy. The idea was not completely new; French historian Alexis de Tocqueville had written of the American genius for naval matters as early as 1836, but the notion that America could make the Caribbean its own lake was something novel indeed.

As they looked around at the competition, these policy makers in Washington saw England as the old and traditional foe, Germany as a new and dangerous one, and Spain as a weak version of what she had once been. If the United States was to become a great world power, based on maritime and naval supremacy, she had best be able to control events in the Caribbean; Cuba seemed like an excellent place to start. This line of thinking prevailed among many Washington, D.C., socialites in the 1890s, where it started to merge with the thinking of yet another prophet.

Born in Wisconsin in 1861, Frederick Jackson Turner lived a life quite different from that of Alfred Thayer Mahan. A son of the Midwest, influenced by the ideals of President Andrew Jackson (who had inspired his middle name), Turner had few thoughts to spare for maritime and naval power. His great thesis, the germ of which was delivered to the American Historical Association at Chicago in 1893, was that the frontier era

CHICAGO IN 1893

Chicago had been coming on strong ever since it recovered from the terrible fire of 1870. Conscious of her role as America's "second" city, and desirous of equaling New York in some capacity, Chicago put on the Columbian Exposition of 1893. It was originally intended to take place in 1892, the four-hundredth anniversary of Columbus's landing, but all sorts of logistical difficulties put the event off until the spring of 1893. When it began, however, the Columbian Exposition was as grand as anything America had ever seen. On May 1, 1893, the first day of the six–month-long extravaganza, 128,695 people were admitted.

The downtown part of Chicago had been converted into what was called the White City. Pavilions, new buildings, and even masterpieces of marble and stone were all constructed for the grand event. Each major foreign nation had a house or pavilion made for its ambassadors, consuls, and trade representatives. Spain had its house between that of Canada and Germany, near the North Pier, close to the location of the present-day Navy Pier.

Replicas of Columbus's three boats, the *Niña, Pinta,* and *Santa Maria,* were built in Spain. They sailed across the Atlantic, up the St. Lawrence River, and reached Chicago on July 12, 1893, the very day that Frederick Jackson Turner gave his landmark address to the Organization of American Historians.

had ended, and with it had passed the first phase of American history.

Americans, Turner argued, had been formed and re-formed, time and again, by their experience of the frontier. First had come the ocean-based settlements of Boston, Jamestown, and New York City; they had been followed by the first tentative moves inland, followed by the great surge of American movement over the Allegheny and Appalachian mountains. "From the time the mountains rose between the pioneer and the seaboard, a new order of Americanism arose. The West and the East began to get out of touch with each other. The settlements from the sea to the mountains kept connection with the rear and had a certain solidarity. But the over-mountain men grew more and more independent."[1]

Today it is difficult to argue with these words. Generation after generation of American scholars have tested them and not found them wanting. In 1893, however, when Turner spoke to the American Historical Association, he was saying something almost brand-new: The frontier had made Americans what they were, in giving them their particular character.

The move over the mountains into the Midwest had been followed by a great surge across the Great Plains and into the Rocky Mountains. By 1848, the United States stretched all the way to California; the discovery of gold in that year prompted yet another influx of migration and immigration. All this movement came to an end, however, in 1890, the year the U.S. Census Bureau announced that the American frontier was closed.

CLOSED?

There were pockets of unsettled areas, to be sure, but there was no longer a distinct American frontier, according to the Census Bureau. From this point, the nation could be considered to be settled, and legislative actions like the Homestead Act and the separate railroad acts would be unnecessary. The United

Historian Frederick Jackson Turner (1861–1932) is pictured here in 1904. In 1893, Turner spoke at the annual convention of the American Historical Association, discussing the end of the American frontier and arguing that "the existence of an area of free land, its continuous recession, and the advance of American settlement westward, explain American development" of its democratic institutions and the habits and character of its people.

States had reached the limit of its internal expansion. Like Alfred Thayer Mahan, Frederick Jackson Turner wrote about the past and he did so in a way that had implicit importance for the present. If the American character had been formed by westward expansion, what would become of Americans once the frontier ended, Turner wondered:

> Since the days when the fleet of Columbus sailed into the waters of the New World [400 years ago] America has been another name for opportunity, and the people of the United States have taken their tone from the incessant expansion which has not only been open but has even been forced upon them. He would be a rash prophet who should assert that the expansive character of American life has now entirely ceased. Movement has been its dominant fact, and unless this training has no effect upon a people, the American energy will continually demand a wider field for its exercise.[2]

Where would that energy go? Alfred Thayer Mahan, the great naval historian, thought of the days of sailing and explained how they had turned into the days of steam engines. Frederick Jackson Turner, the great land historian, explained how the Americans of 1690 had remade themselves into those of 1776 and beyond. Although the two men did not know each other and their work was in different fields, their conclusions pointed in a similar direction: Americans liked to expand, it was in their nature, and now that they had settled the land, they might very well turn to the oceans of the world.

POLITICIANS

As the decade passed its midpoint, America geared up for a presidential election contest, one of the most significant in the nation's history.

Known as the Party of Lincoln, or the Grand Old Party (GOP), the Republicans nominated William McKinley of Ohio for the presidency. He had been a volunteer in the Civil War and had risen to the rank of major, and his life since the war had been both blameless and noteworthy. A man of great personal kindness and sincerity, McKinley appealed to people who wanted an honest man in the White House. He also had the advantage of running on the Republican ticket, a political party that had won most of the election contests since the Civil War.

Democrats nominated William Jennings Bryan of Nebraska. He was young (36 years old), tall, dark, and handsome, and he was one of the finest orators the United States has ever seen. More important, Bryan had a cause: the rural Midwestern farmers who had been hurt by the Depression of 1893. Although he had only a weak grasp of economics, Bryan campaigned with the idea of creating a bimetallic currency, which was one based on silver and gold. In his most famous speech, Bryan cried out that bankers and industrialists would not be allowed to press down "this cross of gold" upon the brows of working men. The stage was set for the most exciting election contest of the nineteenth century.

McKinley, backed by more money and by East Coast interests, stayed largely at home in Ohio, conducting what was called a "front porch campaign." Bryan, eager to win the hearts of working men everywhere, traveled throughout the nation, repeating his Cross of Gold speech and inveighing against the Republican Party. Election Day revealed a nation split, but one that gave the presidency to McKinley.

Bryan swept the Midwestern and prairie states, but McKinley took virtually the entire East Coast and most of the West Coast, as well. Gracious in defeat, Bryan exited the stage for the moment, and McKinley became president in 1897. The two coasts had prevailed over the nation's heartland.

McKinley was a cautious, circumspect man. He made no bold new departures in policy, and he continued most of the policies of the Grover Cleveland administration. In foreign affairs, however, McKinley felt the pressure exerted by those who wanted some sort of action in Cuba, which was torn apart by the revolt that had begun in 1895.

PEARL OR MILLSTONE?

Almost since Columbus stumbled upon it in 1492, Cuba had been part of the far-flung Spanish Empire. At first, the island had been just one of many under Spanish rule, but the introduction of sugar plantations had made Cuba into the Pearl of the Antilles, one of the crown jewels of the Spanish imperial system.

Spain had slowly lost much of her overseas empire. Mexico won its independence in 1821, and most Latin American nations followed by 1840. Spain sold Florida to the United States in 1819, and there was virtually no Spanish political presence left in North America. But Spain held fast to Cuba, the most profitable part of what had once been her glorious empire.

Quite a few Americans, including some major policy makers, believed that Cuba was a natural outpost of the United States and that it should become part of the Stars and Stripes. President Thomas Jefferson was one of the first to suggest this, and President Franklin Pierce attempted to purchase the island from Spain. All efforts were rebuffed, as Imperial Spain hung on to what little was left. The first Spanish-Cuban War changed all this.

The Ten Years' War, as it was called, began in 1868 and dragged on for a full decade. Not all Cubans wanted independence from the motherland; many middle- and upper-class Cubans cherished their political and cultural affiliation with Spain. Yet many Cubans did want independence, and they fought fiercely during the Ten Years' War, which ended in a bloody stalemate. Unable to stop the rebellion, Spanish imperial troops dug immense trenches across parts of the island to separate the rebels from the major cities. By 1878, both sides were exhausted and had little to show for their efforts, so they agreed to a truce.

The United States played no role in the Ten Years' War, largely because its navy was weak at the time. At the conclusion of America's Civil War in 1865, the Union possessed the largest fleet of wooden and ironclad warships in the world, but congressional and presidential advisers agreed that there was no need to keep such a large fleet. Some ships rotted and others rusted, and the U.S. Navy went into a decline that was not reversed until the late 1880s. There was, therefore, no way for the United States to make its presence felt during the first Spanish-Cuban War.

One incident of that long conflict emphasized American naval weakness. In 1873, a Spanish warship chased and caught a smuggling ship, the *Virginius*, that was flying the American flag. The captain was indeed American and so were some of his crew, but they violated international law by using the American flag to cover their activities. Even so, many Americans were shocked when the Spaniards brought the smugglers to trial in Havana and executed most of them. It was around this time that the Black Legend developed, which was the idea that all Spaniards since the time of Columbus were been vengeful, aggressive types who deserved anything bad that happened to them.

Spain endured the Ten Years' War and held on to Cuba, but some—even in the motherland—were starting to wonder if Cuba was worth the price. Was she the Pearl of the Antilles or a millstone around the neck of the Spanish government?

Joining the Navy

The USS *Maine* is one of the most famous ships in American history; but, like many other battleships and cruisers, it took time for the *Maine* to enter onto the world stage. A year passed between the conception of the ship's development and its actual appearance on the ocean.

THE "NEW" NAVY

The U.S. Navy had been incredibly powerful in 1865, at the end of the Civil War, but it languished for the next two decades. In 1885, the United States tried to build a new iron- and steel-clad fleet.

The government made plans as early as 1884, but the battleships did not start to roll off their keels and into the water until the end of that decade. When the ships were completed, American craftsmanship and use of new materials had succeeded in turning out admirable vessels. The *Maine*, intended to honor both the state and the sacrifices its men had made in the Civil War, was designed and built at the U.S. Navy Yard in Brooklyn, New York.

LAUNCHING THE *MAINE*

Approximately 20,000 people came to watch the *Maine* launch on November 18, 1889. They came from Brooklyn, from New York City, and some from farther away. The flood tide was expected at 11:57 A.M., which is when the *Maine* was scheduled to slide off her rollers. There were delays, however, and men working with pumps, shovels, and keels were able to glide her into the water an hour later. The launch was not complete until Miss Alice Tracey Wilmerding, the 18-year-old granddaughter of the Secretary of the U.S. Navy, smashed a bottle of champagne and christened the ship the *Maine*.

Although all of its equipment was not yet ready, the *Maine* was an impressive sight. It was 319 feet (97.2 meters) long, it displaced 6,682 tons (6,061.8 metric tons) of water, and its eight boilers gave more than 9,000 horsepower (9,125 metric horsepower). It had two smokestacks in the midsection and two military masts with fighting tops at both ends. Unlike modern-day warships whose guns are placed on a horizontal deck up front, the *Maine* had two major gun turrets, one starboard and the other on the port side. Theoretically, the guns in those turrets were able to cover a 180-degree span of the horizon. The *Maine* also had secondary artillery in the form of seven six-pounder guns—cannons capable of launching a six pound (three kilograms) projectile. Its normal crew complement was 374 officers and men.

WAR IN CUBA

Not long after the *Maine* was launched and the United States received its new steel navy, the island of Cuba went to war once again. The Ten Years' War of 1868–1878 had solved none of the longstanding issues that bedeviled the island and its Spanish

MAINE, U.S.N.

The USS *Maine* was launched from New York Harbor on November 18, 1889. The ship was commissioned by the U.S. Navy in 1895.

rulers. How was the sugar to be harvested? Who would receive its profits? Was the government to be run solely by Spanish-born *peninsulares,* or would native-born Cubans be included? In addition to all of these questions was yet another matter, one less easily reduced to facts and figures: Many native-born Cubans wanted independence. They were weary of being one of the last colonial peoples in the Western Hemisphere.

Given the proximity of the United States—Havana and Key West are only 90 miles (144.8 kilometers) apart—it was natural that many Cuban exiles would immigrate to America. Miami was a small place in the 1890s, so many Cuban independence *(continues on page 26)*

JOSÉ MARTÍ
(1853–1895)

The Cuban Patriot

Born in Havana in 1853, José Martí was a second-generation Cuban, whose parents were both *peninsulares*, meaning they had come from Spain. Even so, his sympathies were always with the Cubans, not with their motherland.

Martí was a teenager when the Ten Years' War began, and some of his early poetry got him in trouble with the Spanish authorities. He spent more than a year in jail, which he later chronicled in chilling fashion. By the time he was released, Martí had become a devout Cuban patriot, dedicated to the cause of *Cuba Libre* (Free Cuba).

Martí studied law in Spain, wrote poetry in Guatemala, and had an important, though brief, affair with the granddaughter of that nation's president. When he returned to Cuba, he was disillusioned by the state of affairs in his homeland; by 1881, he had settled in Manhattan, where he and some friends formed the core of the Cubans in exile.

Early in 1895, Martí and his comrade Maxímo Gómez sailed from the Dominican Republic to the east coast of Cuba, where they raised the standard of revolt and issued the Grito de Baire (Shout of Baire). We do not know whether they would have succeeded that year because Martí was killed in a heroic, but senseless, charge against Spanish troops. He was buried in Santiago de Cuba.

Like many other patriots killed in action, Martí became a sensation and a martyr to his cause. Thousands of Cubans took up the battle for independence after his death, and he became a symbol to millions of people around the globe, much as the Italian patriot Garibaldi had been before. Today, the Havana airport is named for Martí, and there are statues and memorials to him in Havana, Tampa, Miami, and New York City. Both the regime of Fidel Castro, which started in 1959, and the Cubans in exile today claim Martí as one of their major inspirations.

At the age of 16, José Martí became involved in the movement that led to the 1868 Cuban insurrection. By 1871, he had served a term in prison and been banished to Spain, where he earned a law degree and published poems and essays. When he returned to Cuba to play a role in the new uprising that began in 1895, his life was tragically cut short in a clash between insurgents and Spanish troops.

(continued from page 23)

seekers went to New York City where they created a community in exile, one determined to bring about *Cuba Libre* (Free Cuba).

Early in 1895, some of those exiles went to Cuba and began a revolt on the island's eastern end. Known as the Grito de Baire (the Shout of Baire), this symbolic action started the second Spanish-Cuban War.

Spain reacted with strength. Approximately 150,000 Spanish troops were sent across the Atlantic in 1895 and 1896 to quell the revolt. Some of the best generals went, too; among them was General Valeriano Weyler, who soon won the title "the Butcher." Weyler had served as an officer of observation during the American Civil War, where he had come to admire the scorched earth tactics of American General William Sherman, who had famously said "War is all hell." Sherman had destroyed railroads, bridges, and houses as he marched through Georgia in 1865; Weyler dug trenches across Cuba and set up concentration camps, complete with machine guns and barbed wire (an invention that had appeared in the American West a decade earlier). It is difficult to say what Americans would have thought of Weyler in person, but their impressions of him came from two newspapers that were carrying on a circulation war. When Americans saw the name "The Butcher" in the newspaper, it was good for sales and circulation.

THE *JOURNAL* VERSUS THE *WORLD*

Joseph Pulitzer and William Randolph Hearst, meanwhile, were engaged in a war of their own: They wanted to persuade New York readers to buy their newspapers.

Born in Hungary in 1847, Joseph Pulitzer migrated to the United States in 1864, served briefly in the Civil War, and then moved to St. Louis to practice journalism. Within a decade, he had turned the *St. Louis Post-Dispatch* into a highly successful newspaper and had more than ensured his own fame and

YELLOW JOURNALISM

It is often assumed that yellow journalism had something to do with the yellow peril, which was the fear that Chinese and Japanese immigrants might take over the United States. In fact, *yellow* had to do with color splattered on a page.

Richard Outcault was an American journalist who started to work for Joseph Pulitzer's New York *World* in 1894. As part of the bid to gain the largest share of the New York audience, Pulitzer launched the first full-page comic strip ever seen in an American newspaper. Outcault designed and drew the strip, which included in 1895 the more sensational "Hogan's Alley," a comic strip that focused on the evils of urban life. Most of the cartoon characters were nondescript and easy to forget, except for the "Yellow Kid," who first appeared on February 17, 1895. Sinister and arresting, the Kid was the most compelling figure in the cartoon series, and no matter what the subject of the strip was, it included the Kid, who was completely bald, grinning with two front teeth, two enormous ears, and wearing a large yellow nightshirt. It is hard to say whether readers liked the Kid or were fascinated by his repulsive qualities, but he surely helped sales of the New York *World*.

William Randolph Hearst hired Outcault away from Pulitzer in 1896, and the two worked to create Hearst's new *American Humorist* cartoon paper. Outcault eventually returned to the New York *World,* but by then the cartoon sensation had broken its bounds. From that time forward, virtually any successful American newspaper had to have a cartoon section.

Yellow journalism comes from the first color section done by the New York *World* in 1896, but the name stuck and was eventually applied to all sorts of unscrupulous methods used by Pulitzer and Hearst in the great newspaper war of the late 1890s.

fortune. Not yet satisfied, he moved to Manhattan to take up ownership of the New York *World,* which he turned into the biggest-selling paper of the day.

One can quarrel with some of Pulitzer's actions, but not with his motives. A serious journalist, he believed that an informed public was one of the greatest of democratic assets. Pulitzer's New York *World* reporters and editors brought all sorts of news to the public that had heretofore been kept quiet. Rape, muggings, and break-ins were all reported, but so were election results, corruption in city government, and the need for reform. The result was a booming circulation, and by the early 1890s, the New York *World* was the biggest, most success-ful newspaper in the city and the country.

Born in San Francisco in 1863, William Randolph Hearst was the heir to a fortune made in the silver mines of Nevada. Pranks and practical jokes got him expelled both from prep school and then from Harvard College, but he pushed on to the great passion of his life: journalism and the news. After he led the San Francisco *Examiner* to great success, he came east in 1895, purchased the New York *Journal,* and challenged Joseph Pulitzer for the great share of the New York market.

Pulitzer and Hearst both resorted to unscrupulous meth-ods, but the latter's pockets were deeper. Blessed with an almost inexhaustible inherited wealth and with a consuming desire to be number one, Hearst hired away many of Pulitzer's writers and editors by doubling their salaries. Pulitzer struck back in his editorials, and by 1896, the year that the Spanish-Cuban War really heated up, the two men were deadly rivals in the contest for New York readers. Although no one foresaw it in 1895, the fortunes of both the *World* and the *Herald* would become intertwined with the new Spanish-Cuban War.

Atrocities and Tales Thereof

"I see that we have only good news."
—*President McKinley, to the Spanish ambassador,*
in 1898

There had long been a community of Cuban exiles in New York City. Known as the Cuban Junta, these men and women did all they could to stir up trouble between Spain and the United States, hoping that the United States would choose to confront the Spanish in Cuba.

ATROCITIES (AND TALES THEREOF)

The Cuban Junta did not need to invent stories of atrocities in Cuba. Beginning in 1895 and accelerating in 1896, the Spanish government did all it could to stamp out the Cuban revolt. General Weyler's troops rounded up literally hundreds of thousands of Cuban peasants and forced them into concentration camps. The Spanish government did little to aid the refugees and concentration camp occupants, many of whom perished from starvation, thirst, and yellow fever. Many Spaniards argued that the Cubans brought this treatment upon themselves, but by 1897, it was apparent that there was a full-blown humanitarian crisis on the island.

Hearst's New York *Journal* and Pulitzer's New York *World* highlighted Spanish cruelty and claimed that it was in the Spanish character to act this way. Many American readers believed the Black Legend, which was the idea that Spain was more cruel than other countries and had only wreaked devastation since she first arrived in the New World with the ships of Columbus. Few journalists were prepared to buck the trend, but one did his best. In 1897, a New York publisher brought out George Bronson Rea's *Facts and Fakes About Cuba*. The frontispiece had an illustration of the author, who was sitting under a lean-to somewhere in Cuba. He was being accosted by Gomez, a leader of the Cuban rebels, who warned, "If you or any other American correspondent dares to enter my camp and write the truth concerning our condition, Carramba! I'll shoot you."[1]

Rea's book was long on anecdote and detail but short on analysis. Why were the Cubans in revolt? It is because they were weary of Spanish rule. Were the Spaniards really outrageous barbarians in their treatment of the Cuban rebels? No. Rea did make his desire quite plain. He wrote *Facts and Fakes* in order to "see fair play," and to call attention to "a [propaganda] campaign that has made our press and highest legislative body appear ridiculous in the eyes of the civilized world."[2] It is difficult to say how many people read *Facts and Fakes* or how many of those readers agreed with Rea's interpretation. He alone tried to present a balanced view; most correspondents of the time were, indeed, blatantly on the side of the Cuban rebels and wanted the United States to intervene in the situation.

THE *MAINE'S* NEW CAPTAIN

When we last we saw the USS *Maine,* it was a newly launched ship, operating out of the Brooklyn Navy Yard. Six years had passed, and the *Maine* was now a commissioned man-of-war, rated as a heavy cruiser or a second-class battleship, depending on who evaluated it.

Thanks to the painstaking research of John Edward Weems, we know a good deal about the men who signed on to the *Maine* in its first years of service. They had names like Allen, Bonner, Cole, and Downing, but there was a sprinkling of foreign names among them, including Christiansen (Norwegian), Ishida (Japanese), and Kesskull (German). The maritime section of the United States was heavily represented, and many of the sailors came from Massachusetts and New York, but there was one man from Pennsylvania, another from Ohio, and one from as far inland as Council Bluffs, Iowa. We know that there was a baseball team aboard the *Maine,* and that it had a goat for its mascot. Most important, we know that Captain Charles Sigsbee came aboard on April 10, 1897, the day he took command of the *Maine.*

Born in Albany, New York, in 1845, Sigsbee was a graduate of the U.S. Naval Academy at Annapolis. Young as he was in 1863, he had graduated in time to serve in the Civil War in the Battle of Mobile Bay; he had also been part of the Atlantic Squadron toward the end of the war. Since 1865, Sigsbee had been condemned by peacetime to a long, slow progression up the ranks, like many of his fellow officers. Rapid advancement usually happened only in wartime. He had authored a book on hydrography and had a section of the undersea Gulf of Mexico, Sigsbee's Shelf, named in his honor. When he took command of the *Maine,* Sigsbee was a 51-year-old man, careful and methodical, who had done well in the naval service and who, perhaps, hoped to retire in the near future. (Of course, he made no such statements to his subordinates because that would have encouraged idleness and insubordination.)

The ship he now commanded was a fit example of the new steel navy. The *Maine* was painted white on its hull and ochre on its top parts. It boasted two powerful sets of guns: one on the starboard, and one on the port bows. Although the USS *Maine* was not as powerful as the USS *Oregon*, which was then in service in the Pacific, it was a fine example of American craftsmanship and the power of American policy makers.

The *Maine* had recently returned from a cruise to New Orleans, where its crew had been at liberty to enjoy the annual Mardi Gras. It had been a hit among the New Orleans populace, and the crew very much hoped to return in 1898. The crew and captain alike had to await orders from the U.S. Department of the Navy.

THEODORE ROOSEVELT
(1858–1919)

Young Roosevelt

Theodore Roosevelt is so intimately associated with the Spanish-American War that one sometimes wonders if he had a career prior to the sinking of the *Maine*. The answer is an emphatic "yes."

Born in New York City in 1858, Roosevelt came from a Dutch family that had been around since Manhattan was New Amsterdam, part of the Dutch colonial empire. Although he was wealthy and privileged, he suffered from feelings of inadequacy in youth. Shy, awkward, and asthmatic, he seemed destined to become a rich man's son who would accomplish little on his own.

Sometime in his teens, Roosevelt decided to alter his destiny. He began to box and do gymnastics, and he became an advocate for what he called the "strenuous life," one marked by challenge and cheerfulness in the face of difficulty. By the time he went to Harvard College, he was stronger than most of his peers, and by the time he graduated, he had become something of an intellectual prodigy, as well. His *Naval History of the War of 1812*, published when he

MCKINLEY AND LONG

As mentioned in Chapter 2, William McKinley had won the presidential election of 1896 and been inaugurated in March 1897. History naturally associates his name with the Spanish-American War, but he was the most unwarlike and peace-loving man ever to have inhabited the White House (which was then called the Executive Mansion). McKinley had joined the Ohio Volunteers at the start of the Civil War and served with great honor; although he was never wounded, the experience left him with a horror of war in all its forms. "I have been through one war. I have seen the dead pile up, and I do not want to see another [war]," [3] he said.

was only 24, is still recognized as one of the great works on that subject.

Roosevelt entered New York state politics, becoming first an assemblyman and then the inspector of police for New York City. He brought a swaggering (or bullying, according to some) attitude to the job, but he got things done. Just when things were really going his way, he suffered a terrible blow: His mother and beloved wife died within hours of each other, on the same day. In his diary, he claimed that the light had completely gone out of his life.

Rather than succumb to the tragedy, he left the East Coast for the Dakota Territory, where he farmed and ranched for three years. Locals who tried to intimidate the rich man from the East were soon disabused of that notion, as he proved to be as tough and thorny as ever. By the time he returned east, in 1894, Roosevelt was clearly ascending: He was a patrician who relished the thrill of the fight and a man who was looking for a worthy opponent. Due to his varied experiences as a public servant, writer, and rancher, he in many ways embodied the American spirit of the 1890s.

John D. Long was McKinley's secretary of the Navy. A former governor of Massachusetts, he was popular both in his home state and in Washington, D.C., where his elegant manner and standing in society enhanced the administration's visibility. Long was not in the peak of health, and he often absented himself from Washington during the summer months. During these times, much of the Department of the Navy's business was transacted by Theodore Roosevelt, assistant secretary of the Navy.

Roosevelt was ambitious to the point of aggression. A firm believer in both his personal destiny and the destiny of the United States, he spoke openly of his desire to intervene in Cuba. To do so would enhance American standing in the world and end the humanitarian crisis that was festering there. Roosevelt had a point: Things in Cuba were getting increasingly worse.

Whether one chooses to accept or deny that 200,000 Cubans had already died, as was printed in the major newspapers, it is safe to say that there were humanitarian outrages being committed on both sides. The Spaniards often executed rebels without trial, and the rebels did the same thing whenever possible. Pressure was building from several corners at once, and all recognized a need for the United States to intervene.

The Cuban Junta in New York City fed articles to William Randolph Hearst and Joseph Pulitzer. The American public usually believed what the New York papers said, at least in part because the articles tended to confirm its own prejudiced view of Spain and the Spaniards. Congressional leaders wanted to see an end to the Cuban turmoil, as did American businessmen who feared the results for the U.S. sugar market. Amid all this pressure for either war or for some sort of forcible policy, one person stood strongly for peace: President McKinley. Possessed of great personal charm and forbearance, he held off those who demanded some sort of action. Behind the scenes, however, he determined to put pressure on Spain.

Tough and adventurous, Theodore Roosevelt organized a volunteer cavalry for the war against Spain. Known as the Rough Riders, this military unit was a mix of people that included cowboys, Ivy League athletes, and Native Americans. Roosevelt is shown here in his Rough Riders uniform in 1898.

THE QUEEN AND THE BOY KING

In 1897, Spain was a sad shadow of the great power she once had been. Not only did the country suffer from the efforts to quell the Cuban Revolt, but the monarchy itself was in some danger. Queen Maria Christina, of Austrian birth, was Queen Regent before her son, King Alfonso XIII, became old enough to rule. A gracious, winning person, she felt she could not steer far enough from the reactionary policies of her chief minister. The Spanish monarchy had collapsed once before, in 1873, only to be restored in 1875. The Queen and her cabinet of ministers believed that the monarchy would be endangered if its policies led to an end to Spanish rule in Cuba, still seen as the Pearl of the Antilles. Although the Queen Regent wished to accommodate President William McKinley and thereby avoid war with the United States, there were serious limits on her freedom of movement in the situation.

Antonio Canovas del Castillo, the Spanish prime minister, was assassinated in August 1897, which led to some hope that his successor would be more amenable to agreement with the Americans. But Praxedes Mateo Sagasta, the new prime minister, was also convinced that Spanish popular opinion would not allow for the tame cession of Cuba because the island had a strong emotional appeal for the average Spaniard. The number of Cubans in concentration camps continued to pile up as tales of Spanish atrocities spread. How many of them were true? Even today, more than a century later, it is difficult to say for certain.

PRESIDENTIAL POLICY

Although he is justly remembered as a kind, soft-hearted man (some people of the time regarded him as a saint) William McKinley was also a man of great dignity. He cared about his appearance, his office, and the importance of the presidency. When some members of Congress pressured him and

Though President William McKinley is closely associated with the Spanish-American War, McKinley himself had an intense dislike of war after his service during the Civil War. President McKinley is shown here in this 1899 photograph by Thomas Marr.

threatened that they might start a war with Cuba on their own, he sharply reminded them of the powers given to the president by Article II of the Constitution. He determined foreign policy, not them.

McKinley's policy appeared to bear fruit toward the end of 1897. The Spanish government, led by Prime Minister Sagasta, announced the recall of General Weyler and the partial end to the reconcentration policy. More important, Spain promised a limited form of autonomy to Cuba, which would have representatives in the Spanish Cortes (parliament) and would have its own governing council. These concessions were insufficient so far as the Cuban Junta and the New York newspapers were concerned, but to President McKinley they represented a real breakthrough. Meeting the Spanish minister to the United States, in January 1898, McKinley made a point of saying "I see that we have only good news."[4]

The Winds of War

"Public opinion should be suspended until further report."

—*Captain Sigsbee to Secretary of the Navy*

President McKinley tried to put the best face on it, but American public opinion was turning against Spain and against his Spanish policy. Events at the beginning of 1898 showed that the president was trying to hold back the winds of war.

ORDERED TO HAVANA

On January 24, 1898, the American consul in Havana sent a telegraphic coded message to Washington, D.C., to ask that a battleship be sent to that city. The possibility had been foreseen months earlier, and all was in readiness.

A photo of the USS *Maine* in Havana Harbor, taken on February 15, 1898. A few hours later, an explosion would sink it and kill 260 of its crewmen.

The baseball team of the USS *Maine* was ashore, playing a game, when news came that everyone must be on board at once. The game ended; the mascot remained in Key West; and the *Maine* upped its anchor to head for Havana.

Only 90 miles (144.8 kilometers) separate Key West from Havana, and the *Maine* could have come at night and entered in silence, but Captain Sigsbee decided to make an impression on the populace. On January 25, at about 10:00 A.M., the *Maine* steamed past Morro Castle to anchor in Havana Harbor. Several photographers caught shots of the battleship as it entered the harbor, and it was a fine sight. What neither the photographers nor the Spaniards ashore realized was that the *Maine* was actually ready for a fight; men were concealed inside the gun turrets, in the unlikely event that the ship was fired upon. One of the *Maine* sailors described it in his personal log:

"As soon as it was daylight we could see great hills of the island, almost hidden behind a morning mist. All the watch on deck were ordered to clear away obstructions from the guns and to make the ship ready for fighting."[1] Of course, it was not expected that the Spanish guns of Morro Castle would fire on the *Maine,* but no captain wished to be the unlucky one caught unprepared.

The *Maine's* arrival displeased leading Spanish officials in Havana. Only 24 hours had passed since the U.S. Department of the Navy had sent a telegram saying that a battleship would come, and this was the first arrival of an American man-of-war in more than three years. In all that time, it had been more important to preserve cordial Spanish-American relations; now it seemed that the Yankees had come in force.

The *Maine* was only one ship, but its gun turrets and gleaming white paint suggested both efficiency and strength. The *King Alfonso XII,* a Spanish warship that was anchored nearby, was much less powerful. Even Americans with Cuban sympathies recognized this show of force; some American newspapers showed a brisk Uncle Sam, who came off the ship to be greeted by a rather unhappy Spanish general. "Just a friendly call," the captions read.

It is understandable that the Spaniards thought it was not a friendly call. Virtually all the messages back and forth between Washington, D.C., New York City, and Madrid, Spain indicated that things were increasing in difficulty. President McKinley had indeed assured the Spanish minister that "we have only good news," but even his optimistic account was about to be shattered.

Two days after the *Maine* arrived in Havana on January 25, President McKinley expressed his good wishes to the Spanish minister in Washington, D.C. About five days later came the revelation of the de Lôme letter.

THE DE LÔME AFFAIR

Enrique de Lôme, the Spanish minister to Washington, was a diplomat of extensive service and experience. More than most

PHOTOGRAPHY IN THE SPANISH-AMERICAN WAR

One reason we know so much more about the Spanish-American War than earlier conflicts is the number of journalists and photographers on the scene. Not only were there professionals at work, but quite a few civilians also took photos that later became priceless records of poignant moments. One such photo was snapped on the morning of January 25, 1898, when the *Maine* steamed into Havana Harbor.

Taken from land, the photograph shows two local boys who are sitting on a rock and one lonely boat in the center, while the *Maine* cruises toward Morro Castle. The boat may well contain the harbor pilot, who will take the *Maine* into buoy number four. The scene is rather drab—perhaps because of low tide and brackish water—except for the *Maine,* which simply sparkles in the morning light. The viewer can see the unorthodox rigging of the *Maine*, which has a foremast and an aft mast, with two large smokestacks in the midsection. The hull is painted white, and the upper parts are ochre in color.

Nothing in the photograph suggests that the American battleship is in a state of readiness, or that it is looking for a fight, but we know from sailors' logs that there were men in the gun turrets in case of trouble. The ship looks tight and trim, to use sailors' expressions, and the harbor entrance seems barely large enough to accommodate so large a warship. No wonder those who admired the *Maine* over the coming days claimed that it dominated its surroundings.

We do not know who took this photograph or whether the photographer had any inkling that it would become so important in the record of the *Maine's* short life. We can say, however, that this anonymous photographer has provided us with a wonderful view of how the *Maine* looked as it entered Havana Harbor. The contrast between the very modern battleship and the rather run-down condition of Morro Castle and the lighthouse is remarkable. Many other photographs were taken during the war, which was as well recorded visually as any conflict to date.

Spaniards, he knew of the power and economic strength of the United States; more than most of his countrymen, he wished to avoid war at all costs. Yet just days after he received President McKinley's warm greeting in Washington, the Spanish minister wrote a letter to a friend in Havana. Members of the Cuban Junta stole the letter and brought it to New York City, where a facsimile was released to the press. The New York *Journal* headline exploded with: "Worst Insult to the United States in Its History!"[2]

To say that de Lôme had been insensitive was to put it mildly. In the letter, he indicated that Spain was acting in bad faith, that the promise of Cuban autonomy would not be fulfilled, and that the waiting game had served the Spanish government well in the past. The very worst words, however, were reserved for President McKinley: "[the business] once more shows what McKinley is, weak and a bidder for the admiration of the crowd, besides being a would-be politician who tries to leave a door open behind himself while keeping on good terms with the jingoes of his party."[3]

Whether there was any truth in the statement was irrelevant. Spain, which had already earned American enmity through its treatment of the Cubans, now won American anger by this caustic attack upon President McKinley. Minister de Lôme immediately recognized the catastrophic nature of the disclosure. He resigned immediately and left the United States within a matter of days.

The de Lôme affair made Spanish-American relations even worse than before, but President McKinley, to his credit, did not allow the personal insult to get the better of him. Although there were cries in Congress for war against Spain, McKinley held fast to his diplomatic course; indeed, one could say he showed great forbearance in the situation.

THE FIFTEENTH OF FEBRUARY

Thanks to sailors' diaries and official log books, we know a good deal of what transpired on February 15, 1898. The *Maine* had been in Havana Harbor for approximately three weeks, and despite occasional rumblings of discontent from the populace, there had been no violence incidents with any of the ship's crew. Captain Sigsbee had made courtesy calls to the Spanish admiral and city mayor, and townspeople paid visits to the ship, all of which had come off well.

Most of the 26 officers and 328 men were aboard by 9:00 P.M. Captain Sigsbee was in his cabin, writing away, as were some officers and crew. Many were beginning to snore below decks while others were on deck, on their watches. There was nothing special or different about the evening of February 15. All seemed normal, and then came an explosion.

It was not so loud as it was jarring, and every man awake felt and heard it. Perhaps three seconds passed, then came a second explosion, much louder than the first. Now the ship woke up, with scores, indeed hundreds, of men who were trying to reach the deck.

Captain Sigsbee staggered up one of the dark companionways to reach the deck. His first thought was that the *Maine* was under attack, and his first order was to repel enemies boarding the ship, but there were none. The attack, if it were such, had already come.

Two cadets, Cluverius and Bronson, struggled through water in the hold before they reached the deck. Several sailors were literally blown, by the second explosion, from their posts on deck and onto nearby bunkers and raised positions. Five men in a steam launch anchored by the *Maine* were thrown into the water; remarkably, all five were saved.

Perhaps 10 minutes passed before it became apparent that there was no attack: The ship had suffered two explosions, one coming right on the heels of another. Captain Sigsbee did his best to collect survivors, but he could see that the *Maine* was sinking fast, going down at the fore. He and his fellow officers made their way to the poop deck, a partial deck above the ship's main afterdeck, where a boat was brought to carry the survivors away. The captain was most reluctant to leave, but his fellow officers finally succeeded in persuading him.

George Bronson Rea, one of the few American journalists sympathetic to the Spaniards, was in a Havana café when the explosions occurred. He and journalist Sylvester Scovel hastened to the scene and got into a boat, along with Havana's chief of police, that approached the fast-sinking *Maine*:

> The greatest danger for a time seemed to lie in another magazine explosion; but despite this circumstance, we could see the boats of the Spanish cruiser [*King Alfonso XII*] and of the *City of Washington* darting in and out of the wreckage, bravely rescuing some poor fellow crying for help. We pulled close to the wreck in the hope of being of some assistance. We arrived there fifteen minutes after the crash, the first to reach her from the shore, but in that short time everybody who had survived had already been saved. Too much praise cannot be bestowed on the crews and officers of the two steamers mentioned, who were on the spot immediately after the catastrophe, and their vessels did not draw away for more than three-quarters of an hour after.[4]

Clara Barton had arrived at the Ambrosia Hospital a few hours after the explosions. She found the 30 to 40 men wounded in terrible condition:

> The hair and beards are singed, showing that the burns were from fire and not steam [this proved important in the investigation that followed]. . . . If burned by steam, the clothing would have held the steam and burned all the deeper. As it is, it protected from the heat and the fire and saved their limbs, whilst the faces, hands, and arms are terribly burned. Both officers and men are very reticent in regard to the cause, but all declare it could not have been the result of an internal explosion."[5]

This is a photograph of the USS *Maine* on February 16, 1898, the day after the explosion. Although a naval board of inquiry could not uncover guilty parties, many Americans were convinced Spain was at fault. The Spanish-American War began nine weeks after the explosion.

Captain Sigsbee reached shore that night and had time to send a telegraph to the Department of the Navy: "*Maine* blown up in Havana harbor at nine forty tonight and destroyed. Many wounded and doubtless more killed or drowned. Wounded and others on board Spanish man of war and Ward Line steamer. Send Light House Tenders from Key West for crew and the few pieces of equipment above water. No one has clothing other than that upon him."[6]

Sigsbee then touched on the most delicate matter of all: "Public opinion should be suspended until further report. All officers believed to be saved. Jenkins and Merritt not yet accounted for. Many Spanish officers including representatives of General Blanco now with me to express sympathy."[7]

Would public opinion be suspended?

The Reaction

President McKinley was one of the first to receive the news. For years afterward, one of the White House employees would recount how he had received the telegram with a sense of disbelief, simply repeating to himself, "The *Maine* blown up, the *Maine* blown up!"[1]

AN EYEWITNESS

One of the first eyewitness accounts by a sailor came from the pen of Ambrose Ham, who wrote to his father three days after the explosion. The letter was published in the *Oneonta Star* and then reprinted in the *New York Times*:

> Dear Father: I am well and safe in the hospital at Key West. . . . If I had not been on watch I would be among the

missing, for in the compartment where I slept no one was saved, for that part of the ship was blown up. Whether the ship was destroyed by outside people or accident can only be proved by investigation, and it may cause war. If so, I will do my best to fight for my country. We have taken a great deal from the Spaniards, more than any other country would have taken, and if we do nothing in this matter and let it pass by, we may as well haul down the Stars and Stripes and have no American nation.[2]

Seaman Ham went on to say that he and his fellow survivors would each receive $60 as a clothing allotment, for most of their clothes had been destroyed.

THE NEWSPAPERS

William Randolph Hearst's New York *Journal* and Joseph Pulitzer's New York *World* shared the scoop. On February 16, 1898 the Journal brought out big bold headlines, "Cruiser Maine Blown Up in Havana Harbor." The *Journal* made no secret of its belief that the Spaniards were responsible for the tragedy. The *World* proclaimed "The U.S. Battle-Ship Maine Blown Up in Havana Harbor."

Although these papers are not considered to be objective, the *World* stuck closer to the facts and pointed out that Captain Sigsbee had asked for a suspension of public opinion. The *World* also printed the regrets that Spanish Prime Minister Sagasta sent:

We were grieved and painfully surprised by the catastrophe to the *Maine*. We felt it doubly because the sad occurrence took place in our waters. We cannot forget the sympathy that was shown to us by America when we lost our cruiser, *Reina Regente*, and the Minister of Marine conveyed truly yesterday to General Woodford the condolence of the Spanish Navy.[3]

This is the front page of Joseph Pulitzer's newspaper, the New York *World*, on February 17, 1898. The mysterious explosion of the USS *Maine* was big news.

Plenty of Americans felt sure that the Spanish had actually done the terrible deed, but cooler heads made the first decisions. President McKinley soon learned that 260 men were dead, and although he was appalled by the loss of life, he remained adamant in his course: Peace was still preferable to war. Many members of the press excoriated this attitude, but a memorable sign of support came from the pen of Carl Schurz, former secretary of the Interior. Like President McKinley, Schurz had served in the Civil War, and he had this to say about the *Maine* tragedy:

> What man of good sense and of sound moral instincts would wish that war be resorted to while an honorable adjustment seems attainable? And yet a resort to war is on every possible occasion spoken of, not only by the miscreant with whom the stirring up of a war excitement is a mere business speculation, but even by otherwise rational and respectable persons, with a flippancy as if war were nothing more serious than an international yacht race or a football match?[4]

President McKinley and Shurz were in agreement, but they were losing the battle of public opinion. Americans wanted action, and, quite possibly, revenge.

As soon as the news reached Madrid, the Spanish government issued a series of condolences to the U.S. government and the families of the men lost. Yet some intemperate voices on the far side of the Atlantic, including the recently recalled General Weyler, suggested that it was ineptitude and laxness on the part of the U.S. sailors that brought about the explosions.

THE INQUIRY

Naturally, the U.S. government decided that an investigation was necessary. The Spanish concurred and asked to conduct a joint investigation, but this offer was rejected, so there were two separate boards of inquiry. Assembled on a lighthouse tender ship on February 21, 1898, members of the American court were Captain William T. Sampson of the USS *Iowa*, Captain F.E. Chadwick and Lieutenant-Commander W.P. Potter of the USS *New York*, and Commander Adolph Marix of the USS *Vermont*.

Captain Sigsbee was the first witness to be called. He made a good impression, testifying to the discipline of his crew and the state of order that prevailed aboard the *Maine* prior to the explosions. The board of inquiry naturally tried to obtain information about the amount of coal aboard, the condition of the coal bunkers, and so forth. Nothing untoward appeared in the record. One important aspect of Sigsbee's testimony revolved around how the *Maine* had come to be moored in the first place:

> **Q.** Upon your arrival, did you take a pilot?
> **A.** I did; I took an official pilot sent by the captain of the port of Havana.
> **Q.** Did he birth the *Maine?*
> **A.** He did.
> **Q.** Where?
> **A.** The birth is in the man-of-war anchorage off the Machina, or Shears. . . . My recollection is that the pilot said that it was buoy No. 4. Our bearings, taken soon after mooring, did not place it exactly according to the charted position of buoy No. 4, but no note was taken of this because it was assumed that the charted position might represent former positions.[5]

Although Captain Sigsbee did not make his suspicion plain, it was clear that he thought there was a possibility that the Spanish had moored the *Maine* in an unusual location, one where an explosive might have already been laid.

Lieutenant Holman, second-in-command, was the second witness. He concurred with Captain Sigsbee in all the important details, as did Lieutenant-Commander Wainwright, the third witness brought before the court. Naval cadets Cluverius and Holden, both of whom knew a good deal about the electric wiring system, testified they had seen nothing amiss in the days and hours leading up to the explosion.

By this point in the testimony, it had become clear that there were two explosions, although witnesses differed as to their timing and loudness. The court of inquiry was very interested to learn that some witnesses had seen a great sheet of light appear above the *Maine* just after the first explosion, while others had not. Numerous other witnesses appeared, among them a number of Navy divers who were in the process of exploring the wreck. From the court's point of view, the most important finding was that parts of the *Maine*'s keel had come up almost as high as the waterline and that some of the metal of that keel was bent into a "V" formation. This suggested the work of an explosive device. The court went on to examine many of the surviving sailors, with special emphasis on the five men who had, miraculously, survived when their steam launch had overturned from the force of the explosion. Little new data came to light, and the days were passing rapidly.

PRESSURE ON MCKINLEY

As was shown in Chapter 5, President McKinley was as unwar-like a man ever to occupy the Executive Mansion, which we now call the White House. He had been able to hold off the war hawks in the Congress during 1897 and he had even prevailed over them during the crisis that de Lome's letter caused. Now, McKinley came in for some savage attacks from Congress and the newspapers, and it was uncertain how much longer he could maintain his stance for peace.

Theodore Roosevelt, assistant secretary of the U.S. Navy, took it upon himself to send a very important telegraph message to Commodore George Dewey of the U.S. Asiatic Squadron. Sent just 10 days after the *Maine* blew up, the message read: "Dewey, Hong Kong: Order the Squadron except Monocay to Hong Kong. Keep full of coal. In the event of declaration war Spain, your duty will be to see that the Spanish squadron does not leave the Asiatic coast and then offensive operations in Philippine Islands. Keep Olympia [a large cruiser] until further orders. (signed) Roosevelt."[6]

President McKinley learned that the Spanish were gathering their naval forces in the Azores (off Spain's west coast) and asked Congress for a resolution that would give added strength to the budget for the purpose of defense. Remarkably, the bill appropriating $50 million was passed without a single dissenting vote in either the Senate or the House. The American minister to Spain, General Woodford, reported by telegraph that his Spanish counterparts were amazed by the display of American economic power, for the $50 million came right from the U.S. Treasury; no borrowing was required.

PROCTOR'S SPEECH

On March 17, slightly more than a month after the *Maine* was destroyed, Senator Redfield Proctor of Vermont rose to address his colleagues. A self-made man, brilliant businessman, and a former secretary of war, Proctor had more than average credibility when he spoke on military or financial matters. On this occasion, though, he chose to speak of humanitarian interests, and his finger pointed straight at the Spanish misrule of Cuba.

Proctor had recently returned from a private visit to Cuba, and he assured his Senate colleagues that he had gone with an open mind. He had fully expected, he told them, to find that the talk of hundreds of thousands of Cubans forced into concentration camps was a lie or at least an exaggeration. He found, however:

> Every town and village is surrounded by a trocha (trench) a sort of rifle pit, but constructed on a plan new to me, the dirt being thrown up on the outside and a barbed wire fence on the outer side of the trench. . . . From all the surrounding

These *reconcentrados* are pictured in Remedios, Cuba. Spain's policy of placing native Cubans in reconcentration camps was one of the reasons cited for America's entering into war with Spain.

country the people have been driven into these fortified towns and held there to subsist as they can. They are virtually prison yards and not unlike one in general appearance, except that the walls are not so high and strong, but they suffice, where every point is in the range of a soldier's rifle to keep in the poor reconcentrado women and children."[7]

This was only the beginning of what turned into an indictment of Spanish policy. Senator Proctor had nothing but praise for Clara Barton, the Red Cross, and other humanitarian organizations, but he had nothing but denunciation for Spanish misrule of Cuba. Had he shouted in the manner of a Cuban Junta leader or boasted of American power in the way of a William Randolph Hearst, Proctor might soon have been forgotten, but he delivered this important speech in a calm, dispassionate way. Many people who listened were horrified by the details, and most found Proctor a credible witness. Pressure continued to build on President McKinley.

THE COURT'S FINDINGS

President McKinley forwarded the report of the Naval Court of Inquiry to Congress on March 28. It ran to 280 pages full of details provided by surviving officers and crew, but most of the people who rushed to obtain a copy were more interested in the conclusion, which stated: "In the opinion of the court this effect [on the wreck] could have been produced only by the explosion of a mine situated under the bottom of the ship at about frame 18 and somewhat on the port side of the ship. . . . The court has been unable to obtain evidence fixing the responsibility for the destruction of the *Maine* upon any person or persons."[8]

Public opinion, inflamed by six weeks of waiting for the report, tended to concentrate on the first part of the conclusion and to ignore the second. They thought that it must have been a mine, and the Spanish must have put it there. By now, the calming words of statesmen like Carl Schurz were just about irrelevant; the public wanted war.

LAST CHANCE FOR PEACE

What vexed President McKinley and key members of his administration was the unhelpful attitude of the Spanish government. From the very start of the *Maine* crisis, McKinley

The U.S. Constitution is explicit about the division of powers regarding war. Congress has the power to declare war but the president, as commander in chief, has the power to *prosecute* it.

Some presidents have waged undeclared wars to avoid the issue. This country's first major conflict, the Quasi-War with France in 1798–1800, was never declared by Congress. Other presidents have led Congress and the nation into a position from which war is almost unavoidable; in 1846, President Polk sent most of the U.S. Army to the north bank of the Rio Grande where, not surprisingly, hostilities commenced between American and Mexican troops.

William McKinley was, beyond a doubt, one of the more peace-loving of all American presidents. He held back from war as long as he could, and when it came, he was eager to minimize the loss of life. Yet, he was like most American presidents, both before and since, adamant in his belief in the complete authority of presidential power where war is concerned. It was not for Congress to push the nation into a war, and not for Congress to direct the course of action. These powers, McKinley said, belonged solely to the president.

McKinley submitted his first request for congressional authorization on April 11. This resolution gave him the authority to intervene in Cuba, but it was not an actual declaration of war. He returned to Congress on April 24 with a simple, direct request for a declaration, and he received it.

Congress did muster itself for one demonstration of legislative power. In the debates that led to approval of the first resolution, Congress adopted the Teller Amendment. Proposed by Senator Henry Teller of Colorado, the amendment declared that the United States had no desire to annex Cuba then, or at any later time, and that the armed intervention was only to restore order and government to that island.

had done his best to keep communication channels open and to give the Spanish an opportunity to clear their national name as far as the *Maine* went. Yet McKinley and his chief advisers were thwarted, at least in some respects, by a Spanish government that felt it could make no further concessions. Anxious about public opinion at home and the fragile state of the Spanish monarchy, the Spanish prime minister would do no more than offer promises about what would be done in the future. Cuba would be given full autonomy, he declared, but it could not be done at once.

Could the United States have done more to prevent the slide to war? It was probably not possible. President McKinley had already exerted his will and spent his political capital. Reluctantly, he went before Congress to ask for a resolution to give him authority to intervene in Cuba and bring that island to a peaceful state. Congress happily obliged, and when McKinley went one step further, on April 25, Congress voted to declare war on Spain.

Fire When Ready

"War has commenced between the United States and
Spain."

—*Theodore Roosevelt to Commodore
George Dewey*

From the moment war was declared, all American eyes
were on Cuba, but the first big blow struck in the war
came 10,000 miles (16,093.4 kilometers) away, in a place most
Americans could not even find on a map.

ROOSEVELT AND DEWEY
In the autumn of 1897, months before the *Maine* was sunk,
Assistant Secretary of the Navy Theodore Roosevelt appointed
a new commander of the U.S. Pacific Squadron. Roosevelt had

heard good things about George Dewey's initiative and vigor. Such a man should be in charge, Roosevelt decided.

Arriving at Hong Kong toward the end of 1897, Commodore Dewey worked to put the squadron on full alert. The work of peacetime continued, but there was a definite acceleration in gunnery practice. Then came news of the destruction of the *Maine*.

Dewey had no special connection to the *Maine*, but he may have known Captain Charles Sigsbee from their Civil War service. More important, Dewey was indeed the kind of fighter that Theodore Roosevelt had expected: one quick to get ready to strike a blow. Dewey might have remained at his post for some time had he not received a telegram from Assistant Secretary Roosevelt, ordering him to attack the Spanish Pacific fleet: "War has commenced between the United States and Spain. Proceed at once to Philippine Islands. Commence operations particularly against the Spanish fleet. You must capture vessels or destroy. Use utmost endeavor."[1]

John D. Long was Secretary of the Navy, Dewey's true boss, but he was in Boston when war was declared and Theodore Roosevelt was in Washington, D.C. When Roosevelt sent war orders to Dewey, he ensured that the war with Spain would be a worldwide conflict, with battles that ranged from the Caribbean to the Philippines.

DEWEY AND GRIDLEY

Born in Vermont in 1837, George Dewey was a career naval officer who had first seen action in the Civil War. A great admirer of Union Admiral Farragut, Dewey often asked himself, in tough situations, "What would Farragut do?"

The long years of peacetime had been good to Dewey and his career, but he longed for the kind of action that could earn him fame and glory. In the autumn of 1897, he had been appointed commander of the U.S. Asiatic Squadron, centered in Hong Kong. Just as Theodore Roosevelt had expected, Dewey reformed the squadron, making it battle ready in the days and weeks after he learned of the destruction of the *Maine*. By the time he received his orders from Roosevelt, Dewey's ships were repainted for war (the dazzling peacetime white was replaced by gray) and his crews were in a state of true readiness.

Roosevelt had pushed for an attack on the Spanish Pacific fleet from the very beginning, but President McKinley held off for a few days. The famous telegram, which ordered Dewey to attack the Spanish ships in their home port of Manila Bay, was not sent until April 24. The order came just in time, for the British owners of Hong Kong ordered Dewey's American ships to leave in a show of British neutrality.

By contrast, hundreds of sailors of the British fleet stood silent, at attention, and in full respect for the departing Americans that day. The general consensus among the British was that the Americans were a splendid group of fellows (Anglo-American sentiments had clearly improved of late), but they did not think they would be seen again. Not only did Spain have a longer maritime tradition, but the Americans had no way of knowing where the Spanish guns on land were hidden, or what parts of Manila Bay had been mined.

Admiral Montojo, of the Spanish Imperial Navy, had a fleet that was as big as the American one, but his vessels were in sorry condition and his crews were not much better. Service in the Pacific fleet was considered an onerous chore in the Spanish Navy, and morale had sunk over the weeks and months leading up to the war. Admiral Montojo perhaps knew of the writing of American Captain Alfred T. Mahan (see Chapter 2), and he certainly knew that his ships were not as well prepared as those of the enemy. Yet he would fight it out for the glory and honor of the motherland.

The American squadron entered Manila Bay on the night of April 30, and it moved close to the Spanish fleet on the

An undated portrait shows Commodore George Dewey, who became a national hero by demolishing a Spanish fleet at Manila Bay, on May 1, 1898, at the opening of the Spanish-American War. With this victory, Congress granted him the unique rank of admiral of the U.S. Navy.

morning of May 1. Visibility was not good, and the American ships held their fire as the Spanish ships bounced their first salvoes (simultaneous discharge of two or more guns) too short or too long. The American ships heeded Commodore Dewey's commands and maintained silence until the fog lifted a bit; then Dewey leaned over from his command deck and declared, "You may fire when ready, Gridley."[2]

The words would go down in history as "You may fire when you are ready, Gridley," but the meaning and the moment were the same. Gridley fired a few cautious rounds to locate the range of his guns, and then commenced fire on the Spanish ships. The American squadron steamed through the harbor, circled back, then repeated the maneuver a number of times, with American gunners below decks doing the heavy work. It was exceedingly hot below decks, and most of the gunners soon stripped off all of their clothing. Officers who checked on them found the sailors singing the popular tune, "There'll Be a Hot Time in the Old Town Tonight."

Almost two hours of sustained bombardment did not convince Dewey of his victory until the fog and smoke cleared, whereupon all became obvious. All seven Spanish ships were ruined, and most of their sailors were dead, wounded, or swimming for shore. In contrast, only eight American men were wounded, and one died from heatstroke rather than from gunfire. Dewey had won the most one-sided naval victory of the century; even the British victory at Trafalgar, in 1805, had been much more of a contest.

After Dewey annihilated the enemy fleet, he called on the Spanish governor of Manila to surrender, but his opponent was not yet ready to quit. Annoyed by this persistence, Dewey cut the telegraph cable that connected Manila with other parts of the world, so it was several days before the news of his great victory reached the United States. When it did, Americans went wild with joy, celebrating his glorious victory of May 1, 1898. Dewey's whiskered face appeared all over the newspapers, and some people mentioned his name for president.

A few discordant notes were sounded. Most Americans hardly knew where the Philippines were, yet those islands were now the site of the biggest battle of the war thus far. Had not the war begun in order to liberate Cuba, rather than the Philippines?

MUSIC IN THE WAR

The Spanish–American–Cuban War was so short—approximately 100 days—that very little music was composed for the occasion. Ragtime, a distinctly American type of music, was just beginning to appear, and few "rags" were composed on themes surrounding the war. Some of the most popular of the earlier songs were "Little Annie Rooney," "Sweet Marie," and "The Old Gray Mare," but, fortunately, a new popular favorite appeared just in time for soldiers, sailors, and civilians to sing:

> Come along, get you ready, wear your bran', bran' new gown,
> For there's gwine to be a meeting in that good, good old town,
> Where you knowed ev'rybody and they all knowed you,
> And you've got a rabbit's foot to keep away the hoo-doo.
> . . .
> Please, oh, please, oh, do not let me fall.
> You're all mine and I love you best of all;
> And you must be my man or I'll have no man at all.
> There'll be a hot time in old town tonight,
> My baby!

Composed by Joe Hayden, "There'll Be a Hot Time in the Old Town Tonight" was put to music by Theodore Metz. Authorship was sometimes disputed, as when the *New York Times* reported it had been composed by an African-American woman living in Cripple Creek, Colorado. Most Americans in 1898 probably did not know who the true author was, or even the manner in which it had been composed, but the lyrics and rhythms struck a chord.

President McKinley was thrilled by news of Dewey's victory, but even he admitted he could hardly place the Philippines on a map. Dewey's smashing win placed the U.S. Navy in a commanding position in those islands, but it also raised an important question: Would the United States seek to annex the Philippines someday? McKinley's advisers privately admitted that the matter could become a real challenge, but for the moment, they believed that it was much better to win the Philippines than to let some other nation—such as the British, French, or Germans—step in and take advantage of what had been an American triumph. Meanwhile, the action started to turn toward Cuba.

TEDDY'S ROUGH RIDERS

Just a week after he sent the famous, and vital, telegram to Commodore Dewey that ordered him to attack the Spanish fleet, Theodore Roosevelt resigned as Assistant Secretary of the Navy. He did not do so in a fit of pique or anger; rather, he wanted to prove himself on the battlefield. Roosevelt had been forced to combat his early weakness throughout his life. Boxing had helped to overcome his asthma, ranching had shown he was not a soft easterner, and his actions as assistant secretary clearly demonstrated that he was a man of action.

The secretary of war was quite willing to make Roosevelt the colonel and commander of a regiment of volunteer cavalry, but Roosevelt asked to be made second-in-command instead. His wish was granted, and Roosevelt became the number-two officer to Colonel Leonard Wood, who had previously been physician to President McKinley. Roosevelt and Wood made a splendid team, and they soon formed a regiment completely unique in the history of the U.S. Army: an all-volunteer cavalry regiment of men as diverse as Ivy League scholars, New York City athletes, New Mexico cattle ranchers, and Texan desperadoes. Roosevelt detested the nickname *Teddy*, but he grew to accept what he recognized as a term of endearment, and his men soon became known as Teddy's

Colonel Roosevelt and officers of the Rough Riders are depicted on horseback during Spanish-American War in 1898.

Terrors, the Cavalry Cowpunchers, and finally by a name that stuck: the Rough Riders.

On May 10, Roosevelt arrived at San Antonio, Texas, to find his regiment almost filled. Colonel Wood was already there, and the two men worked fast and hard to whip their recruits into shape. Many needed only a little refining because they were hard workers, whether in the saddle or at the gymnasium, but almost all needed some training in military discipline. As a rule, the men were averse to orders. Two weeks was all the time they had, and Roosevelt, his Rough Riders, and their mounts were on a train bound for Florida by the end of May.

The concern that some felt about how the Rough Riders would be received in the Old Confederacy was quickly put to rest. Town after town greeted them with joyous celebration, and it seemed that many scars from the Civil War (1861–1865) were being healed. By this time it was known that Joseph "Fighting Joe" Wheeler, a Confederate cavalry general in the Civil War, had been made a major general for the new Spanish–Cuban-American conflict. He was the first former Confederate to receive an official commission from the president of the United States.

Tampa Bay, on Florida's west coast, had been selected as the site for embarkation of the U.S. Army. Roosevelt and the Rough Riders arrived in Tampa on June 3 to find a scene of the utmost confusion. The single-tracked railroad line that came into town was completely bottled up, and tons of stores and supplies had just been thrown on the ground because there was nowhere else to put them. The existing supplies were in bad condition, and the poor quality of the meat became legendary among the troops.

It was asking a lot for the U.S. government, which had been made soft by 30 years of peace, to adjust suddenly to the demands of wartime. War had been declared on April 25, and now, at the beginning of June, an army was supposed to embark for Cuba. The army's identity was split into different brigades and regiments, each of which practically had to fight for a place to sleep and for food to eat. Pandemonium prevailed.

Journalists, observers, and do-gooders were at Tampa Bay. Richard Harding Davis, dean of the American press corps, was there. Stephen Crane, author of the *Red Badge of Courage* was present, as was Frederic Remington, the illustrator of so many western scenes. Clara Barton had come, as did members of the American National Red Cross. One could say, without much exaggeration, that the camps in and around Tampa Bay were

HOW ROUGH WERE THEY?

Theodore Roosevelt, writing one year after the war, described his men this way: "Easterners and Westerners, Northerners and Southerners, officers and men, cow-boys and college graduates, wherever they came from, and whatever their social position— possessed in common the traits of hardihood and a thirst for adventure. They were to a man born adventurers, in the old sense of the word."[*]

Few groups from American history are as famed as the Rough Riders of 1898, and with good reason. They were so markedly different from the rest of the U.S. Army; they participated in some of the hottest fighting of the war; and, perhaps most important, many of their actions were captured by the news camera.

Slightly more than 1,500 men joined the Rough Riders. They came from almost all of the 42 states at the time, and from a number of foreign nations too, but Texas supplied the largest single number, with 127. They came from all walks of life, including 160 cowboys, 44 clerks, 53 farmers, and 10 football players (Roosevelt wanted as many serious athletes as he could get). There were furriers, linemen, mechanics, confectioners, and even four congressmen!

When they first arrived in San Antonio, many of the Rough Riders distrusted Roosevelt, for they had the westerner's aversion to people who wore glasses. Roosevelt soon showed them both who was boss and who was a good fellow. He had a natural gift for command, and he soon had them outdoing each other to seek his praise. He concluded his description of the Rough Riders with these words: "Is it any wonder that I loved my regiment?"[**]

---

[*]Theodore Roosevelt, *The Rough Riders: An Autobiography.* The Library of America, 2004, p. 25.
[**]Ibid., p. 182.

the most exciting, though disorganized, places to be found in the whole nation.

General William Shafter, commander in chief of the ground forces, wanted to delay the invasion of Cuba, but pointed, even fierce, telegrams from Washington, D.C. persuaded him to move at once. On June 9, most of 18,000 troops embarked on the ships, which were side-paddle-wheeled outdated vessels that had been leased from private companies for the occasion. Roosevelt and most of his men got on one ship, only to be told that another regiment had orders to board. In typical Roosevelt fashion, he bared his teeth at the other officer and simply said his men had gotten there first.

The bulky, overweight, and confused flotilla put out from Tampa Bay on June 9, only to learn of the possibility that Spanish cruisers were in the vicinity. The flotilla could not proceed, so 18,000 men fried and baked in the Florida sun for five days while reconnaissance failed to turn up any Spanish ships. Then it was off to Cuba, to Santiago, and it hoped, to the success and glory that belonged to heroes.

The Hills of Santiago

"Are we really going into Santiago—and alone?"
—*Clara Barton*

Santiago de Cuba is the name of both a Cuban city and a Cuban province. Located near the southeast tip of the island, Santiago was an Old World city, complete with magnificent ramparts, cobblestoned streets, and cathedrals. In 1898, it was also one of the sites of war.

THE BLOCKADE

The U.S. Navy blockaded Cuba's northern ports within 10 days of the start of war, but it was harder in the southern sphere. Not only was the coastline long, rugged, and treacherous, but the greater distance from any coaling station meant that American ships could not stay long in these waters. The U.S. Navy did not seek to clamp down on Cuba's southern coast until it was confirmed that a major Spanish fleet had sailed from the nearby Azores islands.

Admiral Cervera, one of Spain's most celebrated and honored naval officers, was not at all pleased with the mission assigned to him. Just a few months earlier, Cervera had resigned from an important post ashore because he claimed that it was impossible to bring the dilapidated Spanish navy up to snuff in time for a possible conflict. Now, in April 1898, he was ordered to sail to relieve the Spanish forces in Cuba.

Cervera delayed as long as he dared, for he needed to resupply his ships and to take on torpedo weaponry, but the Spanish government insisted (just as the U.S. government had with General Shafter in Florida), and he sailed in mid-May. The Spanish ships made very slow progress across the Atlantic, but they evaded American vessels sent their way, and Cervera's entire fleet entered the harbor at Santiago de Cuba in late May, unharmed after a dangerous voyage.

The U.S. Atlantic fleet, led by Admiral Sampson, quickly blockaded Cervera's fleet in Santiago, but the mere fact that his ships had escaped harm seemed like a moral victory for the Spaniards. Admiral Sampson sent a few American sailors on a risky attempt to sink their vessel and thereby block the harbor, but the effort failed and the Americans were taken prisoner. Sampson and his ships easily dominated the coastline, but Cervera was safe for the time being.

LANDING THE ARMY

The U.S. Army and Navy had not carried out a major amphibious operation in decades. Although there had been plenty of landings in the Civil War, none had been in waters as truly hostile as those of Cuba, and both General Shafter and the naval leaders were apprehensive. Luckily, the United States did have General García, who was an important Cuban ally.

The veteran of many a skirmish and battle against the Spaniards, García had a very impressive cross mark on his forehead,

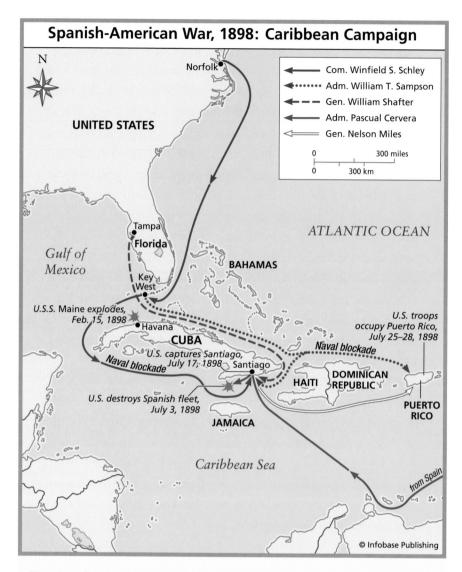

The Spanish-American War was mostly fought in the territories and waters of Cuba and Puerto Rico, the last Spanish possessions in the New World. This map shows troop and fleet movements and major battles of the Caribbean campaign.

made by a gun he had used to try to kill himself while in Spanish captivity. García met with General Shafter, who came ashore for the occasion, and assured the American commander that the coast was not well defended, and that his Cuban freedom fighters would give the Spanish plenty of trouble on their rear flank. Even though General Shafter certainly held the weight of rank and of military importance—he had 18,000 men behind him—he agreed to García's plan that the Americans should make a direct landing on the beaches at Daiquiri.

The landing took place after a naval bombardment on the morning of June 23. To their surprise, the Americans found it rather easy: Thousands were ashore in a matter of hours, and only two men died when their boat slammed against a dock. The Spaniards had evacuated the area well before the landing, which gave the Americans an open road (it was called *Camino Real*, the Royal Road) to Santiago. Yet the first appearance was deceiving. The Camino turned into something of a dirt path, with only room for a few men to move at a time. The Americans had brought a good deal of heavy equipment with them, and it would be hard to carry it up the hills toward the Spanish city.

The Spanish commander had almost as many men as the Americans, but he did not position them all in such a way as to block the land attacks. Because they feared that the U.S. fleet would land sailors or marines, the Spaniards kept a lot of men in and around Santiago. To prevent new attacks from Cuban freedom fighters or guerrillas, he spread his men around the city in such a manner that only 2,000 of his troops were directly in the path of the oncoming Americans. This was a mistake.

KETTLE HILL AND SAN JUAN HILL

The topography of Santiago and the lay of the land that surrounds it can be breathtaking. Due to the heavy moisture of the area, there are large areas of overgrown forest that can resemble jungles, but every so often one stumbles out from the woods to observe spectacular scenery. So it was for the American soldiers, who labored under heavy burdens as they ascended the hills toward Santiago.

A major attack would have been launched as early as June 25 if it had not been for the rain. The rainy season had come and, with it, torrential downpours that soaked all the soldiers through to the skin. There was no relief, and some of the correspondents wired home that the troops showed heroic staying power in the face of this new enemy. The rains continued for three days, and even when the skies cleared on June 30, the paths and trails were still spongy and wet. These were hardly ideal conditions under which to launch an attack, but the high American commanders were nervous. Rumors spread that a large Spanish relief force was heading for the city, and if such a force reached Santiago before the Americans, it might be the Americans who were forced to defend themselves.

Plans were made on the evening of June 30, and every unit had its assignments by nightfall. The entire U.S. Army was to be involved in a major assault, aimed at capturing the range of heights known as the San Juan Mountains (San Juan Hill was just one of several promontories in the area). Just before the mountains came Kettle Hill, so named because the Spaniards had an enormous kettle there to boil sugar. This would be the objective of Teddy Roosevelt and the Rough Riders.

By now, just a week after landing, the Rough Riders had already developed into something of a legend. They were so obviously different from the regular army, and they acted as if they were their own independent striking force. When one Rough Rider carried a message to the commander of another unit, the commander shouted at him for failure to salute and demanded that he act like a proper soldier. The answer was "I'm no soldier, I'm a Rough Rider."[1] His mettle and that of his fellows would be tested on the next day.

The first day of July dawned clear and hot over southeastern Cuba; the temperature would be at least 95°F (35°C). By 6:30 A.M., when the first cannons were fired, most of the American troops had been up for three hours. Exhausted, they had slumbered on the ground for only a few hours before they were quietly summoned for the big push against Santiago. Because of dysentery and malaria among some of the top commanders, the brigade and regimental leaders were shuffled. Colonel Wood of the Rough Riders was given temporary command of General Wheeler's cavalry, and Roosevelt, as lieutenant colonel, had sole command of the Rough Riders, something he relished.

More than 10,000 American soldiers—black and white, volunteer and regular army—were involved in the attack, which was expected to end with the capture of Santiago that afternoon. From the very start, however, the Spaniards proved to be tougher than expected. Not only did they have an excellent position atop Kettle and San Juan Hills, but they used the new Mauser rifles and smokeless powder, which did not give away their positions. By contrast, the Americans had the new Krag-Jorgensen rifle, and many were not equipped with smokeless powder.

Between 6:30 and 11:00 A.M., Roosevelt moved the Rough Riders into position. Although there were many reasons for low morale, the Rough Riders continued on with a stolid determination. By about 1:00 P.M., most of them were in a wooded area, just south and east of Kettle Hill, which was their objective. There was supposed to be covering fire and artillery support, but it proved to be insufficient, and the Spaniards poured devastating rounds of fire onto the Rough Riders. Roosevelt saw one aide killed before his eyes and another one succumbed to heat exhaustion. Some Rough Rider officers—brave or perhaps foolish—were killed because they showed no fear of enemy bullets. At 1:00 P.M., Roosevelt had a united body of troops; one-half hour later, his men were about to break. Something had to give, and he determined that it should not be the Rough Riders.

Roosevelt advanced from the woods to a clearing and found more American soldiers, primarily from other cavalry units. He asked their commander what was taking place, and was told that the order to charge had not yet come. Taking command on the spot, Roosevelt demanded that this officer let his men through. Roused by admiration for the Rough Riders, many of the other cavalrymen joined them in what has been known ever since as the charge up San Juan Hill (although purists remind us that it was actually Kettle Hill).

As they emerged from the wooded area, Roosevelt and his men began to charge, but the word can be misleading. They were actually moving at the double-quick, over very rough terrain, and any sort of open run would have been foolish, for the ground was slippery from the previous day's rain. At this point, Roosevelt was the only man on a horse. He made a splendid target and was hit on the hand by one glancing bullet, but he showed no fear. Neither did his men who continued to advance.

Journalists standing just a few hundred yards away marveled at the coolness of the advancing Americans. Richard Harding Davis reported:

> They walked to greet death at every step, many of them, as they advanced, sinking suddenly or pitching forward and disappearing in the high grass, but the others waded on stubbornly, forming a thin blue line that kept creeping higher and higher up the hill. It was as inevitable as the rising tide. It was a miracle of self-sacrifice, a triumph of bulldog courage, which one watched with breathless wonder.[2]

So many people watched and so many others participated that one can be forgiven for thinking that the charge should be clearly understood and easy to describe, but such is not the case. Just as one photograph or news report never tells a complete story (because the angle of vision is limited), so it is with the charge up San Juan Hill. Some said it was at a trot and that it took ten minutes; others claimed it was closer to a crawl and that it lasted for 20 minutes. What they agree upon is that the Spanish bullets flew the entire time and that the soldiers almost cramped from the severe heat.

Then, it was over as suddenly as it began. Roosevelt and a handful of men made it to the top of the hill and watched the last of the defending Spaniards get away. Other cavalrymen appeared and, within minutes, the top of Kettle Hill swarmed with American troops, astounded by their own success.

ANGEL OF MERCY

The U.S. Army had taken Kettle Hill, San Juan Hill, and almost all of the heights around Santiago, but at a high price. Almost 300 men were killed and hundreds more wounded on July 1. Remarkably, Clara Barton would once more bring relief to the wounded.

Barton had hardly been idle since the destruction of the *Maine*. She had stayed in the Havana area until April 9, and then gone to Tampa, Florida, which, coincidentally became the rendezvous point for all U.S. forces headed to Cuba. A small ship, the *State of Texas*, became the storehouse for the Red Cross supplies, and late in June Clara Barton and approximately 20 other Red Cross personnel sailed for Santiago. They came ashore right on the heels of the first battles at Guanimas and began to tend the wounded and heal the sick immediately. Clara Barton later recalled her feeling when the summons came: "It is the Rough Riders we go to, and the relief may be also rough; but it will be *ready*. A better body of helpers could scarcely be gotten together."[3]

Then came the much more costly battle of July 1, and Barton was soon near the front lines, tending those who had given so much in the charges up the Spanish hills. Again, her own description is better than that of any imitator:

> The road was simply terrific—clayey, muddy, wet and cut to
> the hub. . . . The sight that greeted us on going into the so-

This is a portrait of the *Maine* "base ball club." All members of the club died except for number 1, J.H. Bloomer (upper left, standing).

called hospital grounds was something indescribable . . . a few little dog tents . . . and under these lay huddled together the men fresh from the field or from the operating tables, with no covering over them save such as had clung to them through their troubles, and in the majority of cases no blanket underneath them.[4]

It is possible that Miss Barton sometimes exaggerated in order to get swifter attention from those who sent Red Cross supplies, but on the whole, one is inclined to give credence to her observations. She had known the face of war, famine, and desolation in all sorts of circumstances over the past 30 years. There were some humorous moments, too. On one occasion, she related that a rough-looking man appeared before her and asked if he could purchase some of her supplies with money from his own pocket.

"Not for a million dollars!" she replied.

"But my men need these things. I think a great deal of my men, I am proud of them."

"And we know they are proud of you, Colonel, but we can't send them hospital supplies."

"Then how can I get them?"

"Just ask for them, Colonel."

"Oh, lend me a sack and I'll take them right along."[5]

The colonel was none other than Theodore Roosevelt.

NAVAL GUNS

The attacks of July 1 did not lead the Americans all the way to Santiago, but they convinced the Spanish defenders that it was only a matter of time before the Yankees would prevail. Admiral Cervera of Spain had been in Santiago Harbor for more than a month by now, and he knew the size of the American fleet that lay just a few miles away. Although his chances of escape were poor, Cervera did not want to stay bottled up in the harbor; he wanted to make a run for it. On the morning of July 3, only 36 hours after the Americans took San Juan Hill, Admiral Cervera led his seven ships down the harbor, through the narrow bottleneck opening, and made a run for the open sea.

It was hopeless. Not only were the Americans ready, but they had all the advantages. Cervera's ships, some of them wooden and some made of steel, were no match for the new American steel navy. Just as Alfred Thayer Mahan had predicted, back in March, the Americans had the upper hand in every category. Within a few hours, every single Spanish ship was sunk or captured, and approximately 400 of their men were killed or wounded. American losses were trifling.

Amazingly, the American news corps played a part even in this, the final naval battle. William Randolph Hearst, who had come to Cuba days before, had rented a yacht. He came close to and boarded one of the sinking Spanish ships. U.S. naval officers chased him off the Spanish prize, but he got another of his celebrated scoops.

On July 4, Admiral Sampson sent a telegram to Washington, D.C., that he had a magnificent birthday present to hand the nation: The entire Spanish fleet was destroyed or captured. America was as triumphant at sea as she had already been on land.

NEGOTIATIONS

With the advantage of hindsight, it seems almost inevitable that the Americans would take Santiago. By now, the Spaniards had lost Kettle Hill, San Juan Hill, and their entire fleet. Yet from the point of view of the American soldiers on those hills, the situation was far from rosy.

The Spanish were well entrenched around the city, and the heat was stifling. To ask even the bravest of men to launch an assault under these circumstances seemed foolhardy. Worse, yellow fever had begun to show up in almost every one of the American regiments.

Malaria and dysentery were bad enough, but yellow fever was the great scourge of the time; a remedy would not be found for another decade. So bad did the situation look that Clara Barton temporarily forbade anyone except her own Red Cross staff to board the ship *State of Texas*. This was a poor move from the point of public relations, and one of her leading staff members, George Kennan, resigned in protest.

General Shafter opened negotiations with the Spanish a few days after the destruction of Cervera's fleet, but he found the Spanish commander to be difficult. Cables went back and forth between the American camp and Washington, D.C., with President McKinley's administration pressing for harder terms than the Spanish were willing to accept. There was some apprehension, panic even, among some American troops as the negotiations continued, for if the Americans did not get out of the fever-infested tents rather soon, many men would die.

SPANISH SURRENDER

The Spanish garrison at Santiago surrendered on July 17, 1898. The garrison was permitted the honors of war, which indicated that it had done all it could under the circumstances. American troops took control of the walls of Santiago that very day, but the first ship up the narrow channel and into the harbor was not one of war; rather it was the *State of Texas*.

Even Clara Barton, who was no stranger to the art of public relations, did not expect that she and her fellow Red Cross workers would be on the first ship to enter Santiago Harbor. Later she expressed her feelings as she discovered that her little steamship was the only one heading up the channel to the docks:

> Are we really going into Santiago—and alone? ... Could it be possible that the commander who had captured a city declined to be the first to enter—that he would hold back his flagship and himself and send forward, and first, a cargo of food on a plain ship, under the direction of a woman? Did our commands, military or naval, hold men great enough of soul for such action?[6]

It was true. Clara Barton and the Red Cross were the first ashore.

Peace and Empire

"[Roosevelt] is still mentally in the Sturm and Drang period of early adolescence."

—*William James in 1898*

An American empire was born in the days between February 15 (the day the *Maine* sank) and July 17 (the day Santiago de Cuba surrendered) of 1898. In five short months, the United States emerged as one of the world's most powerful military nations, which caused anxiety about the balance of power as far away as London, Paris, and even Moscow.

HAWAII

No one planned for them to go together, but the American naval victory on July 3 accorded wonderfully with the American annexation of Hawaii on July 6. President McKinley had been in favor of annexation for some time, but Congress had rejected the idea as recently as February. Now, as it basked in the warmth provided by military and naval victories, Congress approved the measure.

PUERTO RICO

Critics of the war—there were already quite a few—correctly pointed out that the official declaration had said nothing about Puerto Rico or any other parts of the Spanish Empire. President McKinley had led the nation to war on a declaration about Cuba and the sufferings of the *reconcentrados*. Now that the war was in full swing and American arms were triumphing everywhere, policy makers like Henry Cabot Lodge and even President McKinley were swayed into further action. Why, they asked each other, should Spain's miserable and corrupt empire continue to hold sway anywhere in the Caribbean? Just days after the Battle of San Juan Hill, American troops were on their way to Puerto Rico.

Thousands of American soldiers landed in early August, but there was almost no fighting. The fight had gone out of the Spanish by this time, and the Puerto Rican population—at least its majority—welcomed the Americans as liberators. Within about three weeks of the landing, almost all of the Spanish soldiers had surrendered, and Puerto Rico had fallen into American hands.

THE PHILIPPINES

Very few congressmen and their constituents had thought about the Philippines prior to the start of the war. From the beginning, the war appeared to be all about Cuba and America's place in the Caribbean. When Theodore Roosevelt sent an order to Commodore Dewey, and Dewey won a victory in Manila Bay on May 1, everything changed. Now the war was as much about the Philippines, 10,000 miles (16,093.4 kilometers) away, as it was about Havana, 90 miles (144.8 km) south of Key West.

As a powerful Republican senator from Massachusetts on the Senate Foreign Relations Committee, Henry Cabot Lodge (above) sought to expand the American military and argued that the United States could not rely solely on its geographic advantages as a deterrent to invasion.

In the same month that General Shafter took Santiago, Commodore Dewey anxiously awaited the arrival of an American land force. Dewey controlled Manila Harbor and all the water approaches, but he had yet to take the city itself. He might have attacked in concert with the Philippine rebels

HENRY CABOT LODGE
(1850–1924)

Roosevelt's "Alter Ego"

There are those who maintain that the senator from Massachusetts practically ran the U.S. government during the late 1890s. That may overstate the case, but there is little doubt that his was the most influential voice when it came to foreign policy.

Born in Boston in 1850, Lodge earned both a law degree and a Ph.D. from Harvard by the age of 26. A protégé of the historian and essayist Henry Adams (they came from the same social class in Boston and Cambridge), Lodge entered Massachusetts politics in his 1920s and national politics in his thirties. Lodge was elected to the U.S. Senate as a Republican, where he was an advocate of the new steel navy and what was called the "large" policy, which meant that American influence should loom large throughout the Western Hemisphere. He was great friends with Theodore Roosevelt and became Teddy's biggest backer during the Spanish-American War. The letters that passed between them provide one of the best sources for understanding the conflict.

After the war, Lodge became an ardent backer of Roosevelt's policies when the latter became president in 1901. Lodge continued to be influential in American foreign policy for another 20 years. In 1919, he led those senators who resisted provisions of the Versailles Treaty that ended the First World War. The result was that the United States did not join the League of Nations, which was created in that treaty.

Lodge died in Boston in 1924. Some see him and Theodore Roosevelt as alter egos, as other selves for each other. There is some truth in that statement, but it overlooks the fact that Roosevelt had much more personal charm, which he used to win people over; Lodge tended to be tough, acerbic, and sometimes downright hostile toward others. His grandson of the same name followed in his footsteps, becoming a senator from Massachusetts, a vice-presidential candidate in 1960, and an ambassador to Vietnam.

(or insurgents, as they were called), but he preferred to wait for American troops. Because so much of the U.S. Army was already in Cuba, or on its way to Puerto Rico, Commodore Dewey got the "afterthoughts"—men hurried from barracks in the western United States and swiftly transported across the Pacific. The men began to arrive at the end of July and in the early part of August. Dewey and the land commander, General Wesley Merritt, felt ready.

The Philippine insurgent forces moved out of the way, by prior arrangement, and approximately 11,000 American troops moved into position by August 1. The closer the Americans came to the Spanish encampments, the more nervous the Spanish commander became. Like most of his men, of whom there were approximately 14,000, the Spanish commander was bone-tired from the war. He would surrender if he could do so with honor; to achieve that objective, he negotiated with Commodore Dewey. The two men knew that for the Spanish garrison to be able to surrender with the honors of war, it had to put up a fight, so by prearrangement, the Americans made an attack on the morning of August 13. The Spaniards fought for a very short time before they raised the white flag, the signal for surrender. Six Americans died and 40 were wounded in the attack (although Dewey and his officers knew of the prearrangement, the other American soldiers did not). Dewey and Merritt's forces took possession of Manila the next day, only to learn that an armistice had been declared between Spain and the United States the day before, on August 12. The fighting was officially over.

THE PEACE TREATY

The armistice that halted hostilities was signed on August 12, but the peace treaty was not concluded until December 10, 1898. There were plenty of steps and missteps in the negotiations, with the McKinley administration insisting on far more from Spain that the original war aims had spelled out. The

Spanish diplomats claimed that the Americans were still trying to pin the sinking of the *Maine*—the cause of which they could not determine—on their government. The *New York Times* responded in an editorial:

> There is no doubt that the destruction of the *Maine* was the proximate cause of the war. ... The President was careful to go no further than he had warrant for going. He did not accuse the Spanish Government of destroying the *Maine*. Neither do the American people. But they do accuse the Spanish Government of failing to protect her and of allowing her to be destroyed. ... The *Maine* was treacherously blown up in the Harbor of Havana while she was under the protection of the Spanish authorities, in circumstances that made the neglect of a precaution for her protection not only an international offense but a crime. That is the belief of the American people. That, they have no doubt whatever, will be the verdict of history.[1]

On December 10, both sides signed the treaty in Paris, under which it was agreed that:

☆ Spain would withdraw entirely from Cuba and renounce any sovereignty over that island.

☆ The United States would receive Puerto Rico and Guam as indemnification for the costs it had incurred during the war.

☆ The Philippines would transfer from Spain to the United States, with a payment from the United States of $20 million.

☆ Spain and the United States would each indemnify their own citizens for any costs incurred.

☆ The Spanish garrison at Manila would be repatriated to Spain at expense of the U.S. government.

There was little mention of the Cuban insurgents or the Filipinos. The treaty made it seem as if the war of 1898 had been strictly between Spain and the United States.

A NEW YEAR

The *New York Times* hailed the beginning of 1899 with a look back at the previous year. Declaring that Americans were a "happy people," the *Times* summed up the events of 1898: "They have triumphed in a war of justice and humanity. They have quickened the lagging footsteps of history, and they have transferred to their own management the affairs of many millions of human beings who have never yet had a fair chance in the world."[2]

The editorial went on to say that Americans were also happy because their material conditions had improved. The United States had gone into an agricultural and financial slump after the Panic of 1893, but that trend now seemed reversed. "Today they are prosperous, they are busy, they are making money rapidly and spending it freely. It may be objected that this is a somewhat worldly and material basis for happiness, but it is real, it is solid. The year just ended has been a wonderful one; the year before us is filled with promise of greater things."[3]

ARGUMENTS ABOUT EMPIRE

There is no doubt that the United States acquired an empire in 1898. What is surprising is the speed and felicity with which it gained lands as far off as the Philippines, as well as a new-found respect from other nations of the world. One surprising by-product of the war was a new courtesy and understanding between the United States and Great Britain. Just three years earlier, the two nations had been in a hostile stance; the American secretary of state had practically threatened war with England because of a Venezuelan boundary issue. Yet throughout the Spanish-American War, the British press was sympathetic, and even friendly, to the American cause. Whether in the

Troop D 5th of the U.S. Cavalry lines up for dinner, in Maya-guaz, Puerto Rico, in 1899.

Pacific or the Caribbean, British sailors testified to goodwill with their American cousins.

To be sure, there was good reason for the new spirit of Anglo-Saxon fellowship. Spain had obviously dropped from the rank of the great powers, and Germany, which had been increasing its military and naval strength for years, seemed to be the next great threat either to England or to the United States. If America had gained an empire, Britain wished to hold onto its empire, and the two English-speaking nations would enjoy considerable feelings of goodwill for years to come.

One Englishman chose to put his feelings into print. Born in India, a subject of Queen Victoria, Rudyard Kipling was as close as one could come to being a citizen of the world in 1899. He had married a Vermonter and lived in that state for several years. Now back in England, he wrote a poem for the occasion of America's entrance to the world stage:

> *Take up the White Man's burden—*
> *Send forth the best ye breed—*
> *Go bind your sons to exile*
> *To serve your captives' need;*
> *To wait in heavy harness,*
> *On fluttered folk and wild—*
> *Your new-caught, sullen peoples,*
> *Half-devil and half-child.*[4]

In other words, Kipling suggested that America do what the British had done throughout the nineteenth century. As the son of a British civil servant, Kipling knew a good deal about the process of empire and its dubious rewards.

> *Take up the White Man's burden—*
> *Have done with childish days—*
> *The lightly proferred laurel,*
> *The easy, ungrudged praise.*
> *Comes now, to search your manhood*
> *Through all the thankless years*
> *Cold, edged with dear-bought wisdom,*
> *The judgment of your peers!*[5]

Like all good poetry, "The White Man's Burden" does not make its case in a simple, straightforward manner, as prose does. Did Kipling really think the Cubans, Puerto Ricans, and Filipinos were "half devil and half child?" It is impossible to say. What can be said is that the poem had an influence on many Americans when it came out in *McClure's* Magazine in 1899. Many saw it as their duty to follow the British in the business of building and keeping an empire around the globe; others strongly resisted the idea.

THE ANTI-IMPERIALIST LEAGUE

Not everyone had jumped with pleasure at the start of the war. Quite a few prominent Americans condemned it from the outset. Most of the audible protests came from New England, where a long tradition of opposition to war had been born during the War of 1812 and nurtured during the Mexican War of 1846–1847. If Theodore Roosevelt and Henry Cabot Lodge, who were both Harvard graduates, represented one thread of eastern thought, then William James and Mark Twain showed another.

Born in New York State in 1841, William James was the elder son of a rich man who was able to indulge his passion for all sorts of learning and leanings. James's younger brother, the novelist Henry James, loved England more than America and spent the last part of his life there. Unlike his brother, William James loved America. As he taught moral philosophy at Harvard, he witnessed the aggressive impulses of the 1890s with severe distaste. James believed in the good that could come from vigorous impulses, but he was sad to see his country become an imperialist nation. This was against his principles and contrary to the traditions established by the founding fathers. At one point in 1899, James lamented to friends that he felt he had lost his country. James saved one of his most severe criticisms for Theodore Roosevelt. The two men knew each other slightly and they might even have agreed on some matters, but in their views of the war, they were complete opposites:

> Although [Roosevelt was] in middle life, as years age, and in a situation of responsibility concrete enough . . . is still mentally in the Sturm and Drang period of early adolescence, treats human affairs, when he makes speeches about them, from the sole point of view of the organic excitement and

difficulty they may bring, gushes over war as the ideal condition of human society . . . and treats peace as a condition of blubberlike and swollen ignobility.[6]

Mark Twain, who needs no special introduction, was in his sixties when the war broke out. He had long despaired of some aspects of American life, most especially the crass materialism that had become so pervasive since the end of the Civil War. Yet Twain was genuinely appalled both by the manner in which McKinley took the nation to war and the ways in which the war was prosecuted. He wrote scathing articles and essays against the war, some of which were used by none other than the steel magnate Andrew Carnegie.

Despite plenty of opposition, the war began, continued, and successfully concluded. By the beginning of 1899, the imperialist segment of American society appeared to have triumphed.

Up From
the Bottom

"There is no evidence that a mine destroyed the
Maine."

—*Admiral Hyman Rickover, 1976*

The *Maine* lingered in the minds of many Americans for a
long time. Perhaps this was because its explosion happened
at a critical juncture, a moment when the United States was
propelled—willing or not—into a bigger, grander vision of
itself. Whatever the reason, it is certain that Americans did not
forget the *Maine* for a long time after 1898.

THE RESURRECTION
In 1911, when Theodore Roosevelt's protégé William Howard
Taft was president, the United States decided to exhume the
body of the *Maine*. Sailors built a crib dam all around the

ship and drained the water out. Observers could see the grisly, twisted metal that testified to its violent destruction. After they were brought to the surface, the remains of the ship were towed out to sea, and then dropped once more.

At about the same time, a second official investigation took place. Chaired by George Melville, a prominent navy engineer, the investigation concluded that the *Maine* had to have been dispatched by a mine from the outside. Thirteen years after the event, the investigation appeared to close the matter for good.

LAST OF THE CREW

In the late 1950s, a number of American historians sought to commemorate the sixtieth anniversary of the destruction of the *Maine*. By now, many Americans had forgotten the *Maine*; its story had been submerged among the bigger, more dramatic tales from World War II, such as stories of Guadalcanal, Midway, and Leyte Gulf. Some people, including John Edward Weems, wanted to bring the *Maine* back to life.

First a newspaperman, then a librarian, and finally a university press publisher, Weems devoted much time in the late 1950s to tracking down surviving members of the *Maine's* crew. Two of the men that he located were Michael J. Flynn of Philadelphia, and Ambrose Ham of Binghamton, New York (whose letter to his father just after the explosion of the *Maine* is discussed in Chapter 6). Both men lived quiet lives, as befitted gentlemen in their seventies and eighties. They had seen the world change a great deal in the years since they were sailors aboard the *Maine*: The world had gone from the use of coal to that of oil, aircraft carriers had replaced battleships, and air power was at least as important as sea power. Yet the *Maine* remained a cornerstone of their lives, as it was—whether consciously or not—for millions of other Americans.

In July 1959, the *New York Times* reported the death of Alonzo Willis, one of the last surviving *Maine* crewmen. He died in Keyport, New Jersey.

Workers raise the wreck of the USS *Maine* in Havana Harbor, on June 21, 1911, more than a decade after the explosion that sank it in February 1898.

THE LAST INVESTIGATION

Almost 20 more years passed before the ghosts of the *Maine* were brought out one last time. By 1976, every man who ever served on the *Maine* was dead, and the world had changed so much that many of them would not have recognized parts of it. Spain, which had languished under the dictatorial regime of General Francisco Franco for 30 years, finally breathed freely once he died in 1976. Just one year later, the voters established a constitutional monarchy, with the popular Juan Carlos as king.

In 1976, U.S. Admiral Hyman Rickover released the text of his report on the *Maine*. Born in Poland just two years after the *Maine* sank, Rickover came to America at the age of six. He graduated from the U.S. Naval Academy in 1922 and rose steadily in the navy, becoming vice admiral in 1958 and full admiral in 1973. An early advocate of nuclear submarines, he was seen both as a visionary and a pest. Bureaucrats detested his tendency to cut corners, and he returned the feeling. In the year or two before 1976 (which was also the year one of his protégés, Jimmy Carter, won the presidential election), Rickover's *How the Battleship Maine Was Destroyed* was published.

THE RED CROSS

It would be nice to say that Clara Barton's fame increased as a result of her actions during the war, but it would be misleading. As skillful and resourceful as she was, Barton was heading toward the end of her leadership of the Red Cross.

Congress voted its thanks, and both the United States and Spain sent her gold medals of appreciation, but Barton's iron-handed leadership led to troubles both during and after the war. Numerous volunteer groups had sprung up around the country, and many of them used the American Red Cross logo without permission and without belonging to the organization at all. Barton was able to stop some of this through a congressional action that recognized the Red Cross in 1900, but she also found challenges within the ranks of her nurses, friends, and even her admirers.

Barton had one last sensational triumph in the Red Cross response to the hurricane that smashed Galveston, Texas, in 1900. By 1902, her critics challenged her within the organization. Led by

With the hindsight of almost 80 years, Rickover was able to apply evidence and interpretations that may have been missing in the heat of the moment, back in 1898. More was known then about spontaneous combustion than had been known in the past, and the record had established a clear pattern of overheating of the steam vessels' boilers. Rickover was particularly interested in the belief—largely implicit in 1898—that the Spanish pilot had anchored the *Maine* in a spot where an explosive device had already been laid. This was highly unlikely, Rickover established, for the Spanish authorities had only learned that the *Maine* would come 12 hours before its arrival, and any attempt to mine that section of the harbor would have

the much-younger Mabel Boardman, these critics persuaded Theodore Roosevelt, who had recently become president, to sever his administration's ties with the American Red Cross. Stunned by this action, Barton hung on for two more years before she resigned as president of the Red Cross in May 1904; she was then 83 years old.

The Red Cross was reorganized over the next few years, with many of Barton's former critics now in leadership positions. Caustic and sometimes bitter, she watched from the sidelines, as they succeeded in making the American Red Cross part of the International Red Cross—something she had wanted but had been unable to accomplish. Barton died in 1912, at the age of 90.

Barton was a one-of-a-kind dynamo of activity who had almost single-handedly created an organization. Her actions in Cuba had been creditable, and she lasted far longer than is the case with many founders. Like some other natural leaders, she was far better at inspiring and acting than in the day-to-day operation of an organization.

This American Red Cross poster (circa 1914) encourages citizens to join the organization in order to serve humanity.

attracted a good deal of attention. His conclusion, reached after exhaustive work, was simple and to the point: "There is no evidence that a mine destroyed the *Maine*."[1]

One can certainly ask a counterquestion: Would it have mattered if people had known this in 1898? Although no one can say for certain, it seems likely that the impetus to war had been created in the weeks and months prior to the *Maine's* arrival in Havana Harbor. It is difficult for us to imagine a scenario in which the United States and Spanish governments agreed to an indemnity and the matter was then closed.

THE SHIP AND THE WAR

By the middle of the twentieth century, the *Maine* and the Spanish-American War became fused in the minds of most Americans. School children routinely learned that the *Maine* had been blown up in Havana Harbor, but with little context about the Spanish-Cuban War or the humanitarian issues that existed in Cuba at the time. Some of this was perfectly natural; just as Americans put Pearl Harbor and World War II together, they join the sinking of the *Maine* and the Spanish-American War. It is important to remember, however, that the ship and even its explosion did not cause the war. Many factors led to the Spanish-American War, and it is quite possible that it would have happened even without the explosion of the *Maine*. It is beyond a doubt, however, that the ship's destruction hastened the start of the war.

CHRONOLOGY

1868   Ten Years' War between Cuba and Spain begins.

1873   Americans are executed as a result of the *Virginius* Affair; new U.S. steel-hulled navy proposed.

1889   **November 18** USS *Maine* is launched; 20,000 people come to watch.

1890   Alfred T. Mahan's *The Influence of Sea Power upon History* is published; USS *Maine* launched at Brooklyn

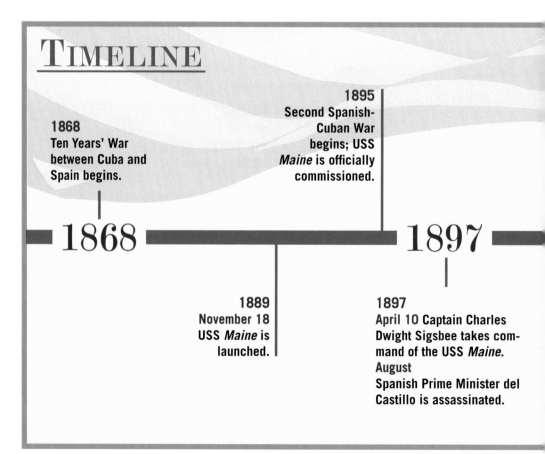

TIMELINE

1868
Ten Years' War between Cuba and Spain begins.

1895
Second Spanish-Cuban War begins; USS *Maine* is officially commissioned.

1868

1897

1889
November 18 USS *Maine* is launched.

1897
April 10 Captain Charles Dwight Sigsbee takes command of the USS *Maine*.
August
Spanish Prime Minister del Castillo is assassinated.

Navy Yard; U.S. Census Bureau declares American frontier is closed; the Gay Nineties begin.

1892   World's Fair and Columbian Exposition opens in Chicago.

1893   Replicas of Columbus's ships arrive at Columbian Exposition; Frederick Jackson Turner delivers address on the significance of the frontier in American history in Chicago.

1895   Second Spanish-Cuban War begins; William Randolph Hearst purchases the New York *Journal*; USS *Maine* is officially commissioned.

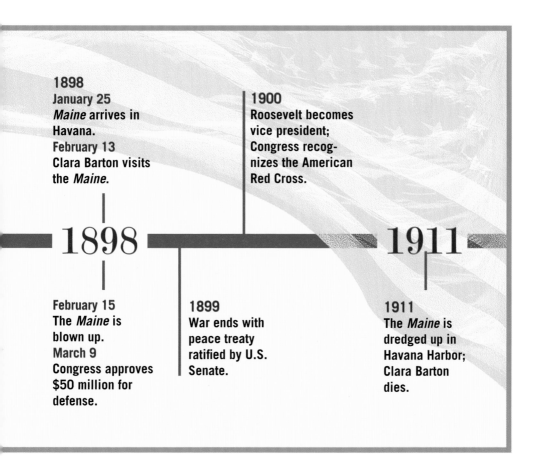

1898
January 25
Maine arrives in Havana.
February 13
Clara Barton visits the *Maine*.

1900
Roosevelt becomes vice president; Congress recognizes the American Red Cross.

1898

1911

February 15
The *Maine* is blown up.
March 9
Congress approves $50 million for defense.

1899
War ends with peace treaty ratified by U.S. Senate.

1911
The *Maine* is dredged up in Havana Harbor; Clara Barton dies.

1896   The "Yellow Kid" first appears in the New York *World*; William McKinley defeats William Jennings Bryan in presidential election; Spain begins policy of reconcentration camps.

1897   McKinley inaugurated; Clara Barton, who turns 76, decides to go to Cuba.

April 10 Captain Charles Dwight Sigsbee takes command of the USS *Maine*.

August Spanish Prime Minister del Castillo is assassinated.

1898   **January 24** The *Maine* is ordered to leave for Havana.

January 25 *Maine* arrives in Havana.

February 9 Clara Barton arrives in Havana.

February 13 Barton visits the *Maine*.

February 15 The *Maine* is blown up.

March 9 Congress approves $50 million for defense.

March 17 Senator Proctor addresses the U.S. Senate.

April 9 Clara Barton leaves Havana.

April 11 McKinley asks for congressional authorization to act in Cuba.

April 25 Congress declares war.

May 1 Admiral Dewey destroys Spanish fleet in Manila Bay.

May 10 Theodore Roosevelt arrives in San Antonio.

June 9 American troops board in Tampa, Florida.

June 20 Clara Barton and Red Cross sail from Tampa Bay.

June 23 Americans land near Santiago.

July 1 Battles of Kettle Hill and San Juan Hill occur.

July 2 Clara Barton meets Theodore Roosevelt behind the lines.

July 3 American fleet destroys Spanish fleet of Admiral Cervera.

July 6 The United States formally annexes Hawaii.

July 17 Santiago surrenders.

July 18 Clara Barton enters Santiago Harbor.

August 12 Armistice is signed.

August 13 Manila surrenders.

December 10 Peace treaty is signed.

1899   War ends with peace treaty ratified by U.S. Senate.

1900   Roosevelt becomes vice president; Congress recognizes the American Red Cross.

1901   Upon the assassination of William McKinley, Roosevelt becomes president.

1904   **May** Clara Barton resigns as president of Red Cross.

1911   The *Maine* is dredged up in Havana Harbor; Clara Barton dies.

1960   Last living member of the *Maine* crew dies.

1976   Admiral Hyman Rickover publishes his study of the *Maine* explosion.

NOTES

CHAPTER 1

1. U.S. Navy Department, *The Report of the Naval Court of Inquiry upon the Destruction of the United States Battle Ship Maine.* Washington D.C.: Government Print Office, 1898, p. 15.
2. William E. Barton, *The Life of Clara Barton, Founder of the American Red Cross.* Houghton Mifflin, 1922, p. 285.
3. George Bronson Rea, "The Night of the Explosion in Havana," *Harper's Weekly.* (March 5, 1898)."
4. Ibid.
5. William E. Barton, *The Life of Clara Barton,* pp. 285–286.
6. Elizabeth Brown Pryor, *Clara Barton, Professional Angel.* University of Pennsylvania Press, 1987, p. 303.
7. William E. Barton, *The Life of Clara Barton,* p. 284.

CHAPTER 2

1. Frederick Jackson Turner, *The Frontier in American History.* New York: Henry Holt, 1920, p. 18.
2. Ibid., p. 37.

CHAPTER 4

1. George Bronson Rea, *Facts and Fakes About Cuba.* New York: George Munro's Sons, 1897. 2. Ibid., p. 30.

3. H. Wayne Morgan, *William McKinley and His America.* Kent, Ohio: Kent State University Press, 2003, p. 274.
4. Ibid., p. 269.

CHAPTER 5

1. John Edward Weems, *The Fate of the Maine: The Biography of a Celebrated Ship.* New York: Henry Holt, 1958, pp. 48–49.
2. CITE INFO TK
3. Morgan, *William McKinley and His America,* p. 270.
4. Rea, "The Night of the Explosion in Havana."
5. William E. Barton, *The Life of Clara Barton,* p. 286.
6. Michael Blow, *A Ship to Remember: The Maine and the Spanish-American War.* New York: William Morrow, 1992, pp. 101–102.
7. Ibid., p. 102.

CHAPTER 6

1. Morgan, *William McKinley and His America,* p. 273.
2. "Routine Duty on the Maine: One of the Ship's Company," *New York Times.* (February 25, 1898): p. 2.
3. "Sagasta Sends Through the World Spain's Sympathy," *New York World.* (February 18, 1898).
4. Carl Shurz, "About War," *Harper's Weekly.* (March 5, 1898).

5. U.S. Navy Department, *The Report of the Naval Court of Inquiry*, p. 10.
6. Frank Freidel, *The Splendid Little War*. New York: Little, Brown 1958, p. 14.
7. Proctor
8. U.S. Navy Department, *The Report of the Naval Court of Inquiry*, p. 56.

CHAPTER 7

1. Freidel, *The Splendid Little War*, p.
2. G.J.A. O'Toole, *The Spanish War: An American Epic, 1898*. New York: Norton, 1984, p. 174.

CHAPTER 8

1. Virgil Carrington Jones, *Roosevelt's Rough Riders*. Garden City, N.Y.: Doubleday, 1971.
2. Ibid., p. 183.
3. Clara Barton, *The Red Cross*. Washington D.C.: American National Red Cross, 1898, p. 557.
4. Ibid., p. 564.

5. Percy H. Epler, *The Life of Clara Barton*. New York: Macmillan, 1915, pp. 299–300.
6. Ibid., p. 309.

CHAPTER 9

1. "Spain and the Maine," *New York Times*. (December 10, 1898): p. 8.
2. "A Happy People," *New York Times*. (January 1, 1899): p. 17.
3. Ibid.
4. "The White Man's Burden," http://en.wikipedia.org/wiki/The_White_Man's_Burden.
5. Ibid.
6. Robert L. Beisner, *Twelve Against Empire: The Anti-imperialists, 1898–1900*. New York: McGraw Hill, 1968, p. 43.

CHAPTER 10

1. H.G. Rickover, *How the Battleship Maine Was Destroyed*. Washington, D.C.: Naval History Division, 1976, p. 91.

BIBLIOGRAPHY

Barton, Clara. *The Red Cross.* Washington D.C.: American National Red Cross, 1898.

Barton, William E. *The Life of Clara Barton, Founder of the American Red Cross.* Houghton Mifflin, 1922.

Beisner, Robert L. *Twelve Against Empire: The Anti-Imperialists, 1898–1900.* New York: McGraw-Hill, 1968.

Blow, Michael. *A Ship to Remember: The Maine and the Spanish-American War.* New York: William Morrow, 1992.

Epler, Percy H. *The Life of Clara Barton.* New York: Macmillan, 1915.

Estrada, Alfredo José. *Havana: Autobiography of a City.* New York: Palgrave Macmillan, 2007.

Freidel, Frank. *The Splendid Little War.* New York: Little, Brown, 1958.

Jones, Virgil Carrington. *Roosevelt's Rough Riders.* Garden City, N.Y.: Doubleday, 1971.

Morgan, H. Wayne. *William McKinley and His America.* Kent, Ohio: Kent State University Press, 2003.

O'Toole, G.J.A. *The Spanish War: An American Epic, 1898.* New York: Norton, 1984.

Phillips, Kevin. *William McKinley.* New York: Times Books, 2003.

Pryor, Elizabeth Brown. *Clara Barton, Professional Angel.* Philadelphia: University of Pennsylvania Press, 1987.

Rea, George Bronson. *Facts and Fakes About Cuba.* New York: George Munro's Sons, 1897.

Rickover H.G. *How the Battleship* Maine *Was Destroyed.* Washington, D.C.: Naval History Division, 1976.

Traxel, David. *1898.* New York: Knopf, 1998.

Turner, Frederick Jackson. *The Frontier in American History.* New York: Henry Holt, 1920.

U.S. Navy Department. *The Report of the Naval Court of Inquiry upon the Destruction of the United States Battle Ship* Maine. Washington D.C.: Government Print Office, 1898.

Weems, John Edward. *The Fate of the* Maine: *The Biography of a Celebrated Ship.* New York: Henry Holt, 1958.

Further Reading

Blow, Michael. *A Ship to Remember: The* Maine *and the Spanish-American War.* New York: William Morrow, 1992.

Estrada, Alfredo José. *Havana: Autobiography of a City.* New York: Palgrave Macmillan, 2007.

Freidel, Frank. *The Splendid Little War.* New York: Little, Brown, 1958.

Jones, Virgil Carrington. *Roosevelt's Rough Riders.* Garden City, N.Y.: Doubleday, 1971.

Post, Charles Johnson. *The Little War of Private Post.* New York: Little, Brown, 1960.

Weems, John Edward. *The Fate of the* Maine: *The Biography of a Celebrated Ship.* New York: Henry Holt, 1958.

WEB SITES

"Crew Roster—USS *Maine*," The Spanish-American War, Centennial Web site

http://www.spanamwar.com/mainecrw.htm

"Cuba Travel Photos," Cuba-Pictures.com

http://cuba-pictures.com/

"Medicine in the Spanish-American War," The Spanish-American War, Centennial Web site

http://www.spanamwar.com/medical.htm

"The Spanish-American War." The Spanish-American War, Centennial Web site

http://www.spanamwar.com

"Yellow Journalism," PBS.org

http://www.pbs.org/crucible/journalism.html

Photo Credits

INDEX

ABOUT THE AUTHOR

SAMUEL WILLARD CROMPTON has been interested in ships since his teenage years, when he built models of the *Golden Hind*, the *Bounty*, and the USS *Constitution*. He is the author of *Sinking of the Bismarck*, also by Chelsea House, and was a member of the National Endowment for the Humanties program "The American Maritime People" at Mystic Seaport in 2006. Crompton lives and works in the Berkshire Hills of western Massachusetts.